16LIVES

MICHAEL MALLIN

The 16LIVES series

BRIAN HUGHES

Brian Hughes was born in Dublin and studied in NUI Maynooth where he graduated with a BA in History and English. He received an M.Phil in Modern Irish History from Trinity College, Dublin, where he wrote a dissertation on Michael Mallin. He is currently working on a PhD thesis on the Irish revolution.

LORCAN COLLINS – SERIES EDITOR

LORCAN COLLINS Co-author, with Conor Kostick, of *The Easter Rising*; founder of the 1916 Rebellion Walking Tour of Dublin; author of *James Connolly* in the 16 Lives series and *1916:The Rising Handbook*. He lectures on 1916 in the US, and is a contributor to historical journals, radio and TV.

DR RUÁN O'DONNELL – SERIES EDITOR

RUÁN O'DONNELL Senior Lecturer, history department, University of Limerick; books include *Robert Emmet and the Rising of 1803*, *The Impact of the 1916 Rising* (ed.), *Special Category:The IRA in English Prisons, 1968–1978* and *1978–1985*, and *The O'Brien Pocket History of the Irish Famine*.

16LIVES

MICHAEL MALLIN

Brian Hughes

THE O'BRIEN PRESS
DUBLIN

First published 2012 by
The O'Brien Press Ltd,
12 Terenure Road East, Rathgar,
Dublin 6, D06 HD27, Ireland.
Tel: +353 1 4923333; Fax: +353 1 4922777
E-mail: books@obrien.ie.
Website: www.obrien.ie
Reprinted 2016.

ISBN: 978-1-84717-266-2

PICTURE CREDITS
The author and publisher thank the following for permission to use photographs and
illustrative material:
front cover image: Kilmainham Gaol Collection; back cover: Kilmainham Gaol; inside
front cover: Kilmainham Gaol;
Kilmainham Gaol Collection: section 1, p1, p2 both, p3 all, p6 top, p7 bottom, p8 bottom; section 2: p3 top, p4 bottom, p5 bottom, p7 bottom, p8; Lorcan Collins: section 1,
p4 both, p5 top, p7 top, p8 top; section 2: p3 bottom, p4 top, p5 top; NLI: section 1, p5
bottom, p6 bottom; RTE: section 2, p1 top, p7 top; Royal College of Surgeons in Ireland:
section 2, p1 bottom, p2 both; Honor O Brolchain: section 2, p6.
If any involuntary infringement of copyright has occurred, sincere apologies are offered
and the owners of such copyright are requested to contact the publisher.

10 9 8 7 6 5 4 3 2
21 20 19 18 17 16

Printed and bound by CPI Group (UK) Ltd, Croydon, CR0 4YY
The paper used in this book is produced using pulp from managed forests.

Published in:

DUBLIN

UNESCO
City of Literature

DEDICATION

To my parents

ACKNOWLEDGEMENTS

This project started life in 2007 as a dissertation for an M.Phil in Modern Irish History in Trinity College, Dublin. That dissertation was completed in 2008 under the supervision of Dr Anne Dolan. I owe a huge debt of gratitude to Dr Dolan who was, and continues to be, a source of advice, encouragement and inspiration to my research.

My name would not be on this book were it not for Lorcan Collins, creator and co-editor of the Sixteen Lives series. Lorcan has shown a great amount of faith in me and for that I am eternally grateful. As well as shepherding me along on this project, Lorcan also sourced many of the brilliant photographs that are reproduced in this book.

At the O'Brien Press I am indebted to Michael O'Brien for the opportunity. I am grateful to my editor Ide Ní Laoghaire and designer Emma Byrne whose expertise and professionalism is evident throughout the book.

A number of friends read extracts and chapters at various stages of the book's life and I am most grateful to them all: Conor Mackey, Fergal O'Leary, Ian Priestley, Rita Murray, Jürgen Karwig and Amy Branagan. James Buckley has proofread, provided feedback and a keen and interested ear since I began writing about Michael Mallin and deserves special thanks. Fr Joseph Mallin, Michael Mallin's son, has been an inspiration and provided invaluable information in his many wonderful letters. Other relatives of Mallin – Niall O Callanain, Una Ui Cheallanain and Sean Tapley – have also been very kind in dealing with my questions. I thank Francis Devine for information and membership numbers for the Silk Weavers' Union, and Denis Condon on Dublin cinema.

I would like to thank the archivists and staff at the National Library of Ireland, National Archives, Dublin, the Allen Library and Trinity College Library for their help during my research. I wish to pay particular thanks to those who helped source and provided permission for reproduction of photographs, in particular Niall Bergin and Anne-Marie Ryan of the Kilmainham Gaol museum and June Shannon and Mary O'Doherty of the Royal College of Surgeons of Ireland.

Finally, I wish to place on record my deep gratitude to my parents, Seamus and Jacinta, who have been fully supportive of everything I have done or tried to do. This book is for them.

16LIVES Timeline

1845–51. The Great Hunger in Ireland. One million people die and over the next decades millions more emigrate.

1858, March 17. The Irish Republican Brotherhood, or Fenians, are formed with the express intention of overthrowing British rule in Ireland by whatever means necessary.

1867, February and March. Fenian Uprising.

1870, May. Home Rule movement, founded by Isaac Butt, who had previously campaigned for amnesty for Fenian prisoners.

1879–81. The Land War. Violent agrarian agitation against English landlords.

1884, November 1. The Gaelic Athletic Association founded – immediately infiltrated by the Irish Republican Brotherhood (IRB).

1893, July 31. Gaelic League founded by Douglas Hyde and Eoin MacNeill. The Gaelic Revival, a period of Irish Nationalism, pride in the language, history, culture and sport.

1900, September. Cumann na nGaedheal (Irish Council) founded by Arthur Griffith.

1905–07. Cumann na nGaedheal, the Dungannon Clubs and the National Council are amalgamated to form Sinn Féin (We Ourselves).

1909, August. Countess Markievicz and Bulmer Hobson organise nationalist youths into Na Fianna Éireann (Warriors of Ireland) a kind of boy scout brigade.

1912, April. Prime minister Asquith introduces the Third Home Rule Bill to the British Parliament. Passed by the Commons and rejected by the Lords, the Bill would have to become law due to the Parliament Act. Home Rule expected to be introduced for Ireland by autumn 1914.

1913, January. Sir Edward Carson and James Craig set up Ulster Volunteer Force (UVF) with the intention of defending Ulster against Home Rule.

1913. Jim Larkin, founder of the Irish Transport and General Workers' Union (ITGWU), calls for a workers' strike for better pay and conditions.

1913, August 31. Jim Larkin speaks at a banned rally on Sackville Street; Bloody Sunday.

1913, November 23. James Connolly, Jack White and Jim Larkin establish the Irish Citizen Army (ICA) in order to protect strikers.

1913, November 25. The Irish Volunteers founded in Dublin to 'secure the rights and liberties common to all the people of Ireland'.

1914, March 20. Resignations of British officers force British government not to use British army to enforce Home Rule, an event known as the 'Curragh Mutiny'.

1914, April 2. In Dublin, Agnes O'Farrelly, Mary MacSwiney, Countess Markievicz and others establish Cumann na mBan as a women's volunteer force dedicated to establishing Irish freedom and assisting the Irish Volunteers.

1914, April 24. A shipment of 35,000 rifles and five million rounds of ammunition is landed at Larne for the UVF.

1914, July 26. Irish Volunteers unload a shipment of 900 rifles and 45,000 rounds of ammunition shipped from Germany aboard Erskine Childers' yacht, the *Asgard*. British troops fire on crowd on Bachelors Walk, Dublin. Three citizens are killed.

1914, August 4. Britain declares war on Germany. Home Rule for Ireland shelved for the duration of the First World War.

1914, September 9. Meeting held at Gaelic League headquarters between IRB and other extreme republicans. Initial decision made to stage an uprising while Britain is at war.

1914, September. 170,000 leave the Volunteers and form the National Volunteers or Redmondites. Only 11,000 remain as the Irish Volunteers under Eoin MacNeill.

1915, May–September. Military Council of the IRB is formed.

1915, August 1. Pearse gives fiery oration at the funeral of Jeremiah O'Donovan Rossa.

1916, January 19–22. James Connolly joins the IRB Military Council, thus ensuring that the ICA shall be involved in the Rising. Rising date confirmed for Easter.

1916, April 20, 4.15pm. The *Aud* arrives at Tralee Bay, laden with 20,000 German rifles for the Rising. Captain Karl Spindler waits in vain for a signal from shore.

1916, April 21, 2.15am. Roger Casement and his two companions go ashore from U-19 and land on Banna Strand. Casement is arrested at McKenna's Fort.

6.30pm. The *Aud* is captured by the British navy and forced to sail towards Cork harbour.

22 April, 9.30am. The *Aud* is scuttled by her captain off Daunt's Rock.

10pm. Eoin MacNeill as Chief-of-Staff of the Irish Volunteers issues the countermanding order in Dublin to try to stop the Rising.

1916, April 23, 9am, Easter Sunday. The Military Council meets to discuss the situation, considering MacNeill has placed an advertisement in a Sunday newspaper halting all Volunteer operations. The Rising is put on hold for twenty-four hours. Hundreds of copies of the Proclamation of the Irish Republic are printed in Liberty Hall.

1916, April 24, 12 noon, Easter Monday. The Rising begins in Dublin.

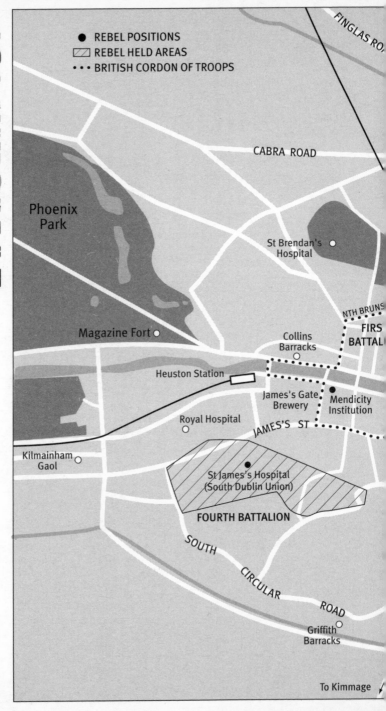

16LIVESMAP

REBEL POSITIONS
REBEL HELD AREAS
BRITISH CORDON OF TROOPS

FINGLAS RO

CABRA ROAD

Phoenix Park

St Brendan's Hospital

NTH BRUNS

Magazine Fort

Collins Barracks

FIRS BATTAL

Heuston Station

James's Gate Brewery

Mendicity Institution

Royal Hospital

JAMES'S ST

Kilmainham Gaol

St James's Hospital (South Dublin Union)

FOURTH BATTALION

SOUTH

CIRCULAR

ROAD

Griffith Barracks

To Kimmage

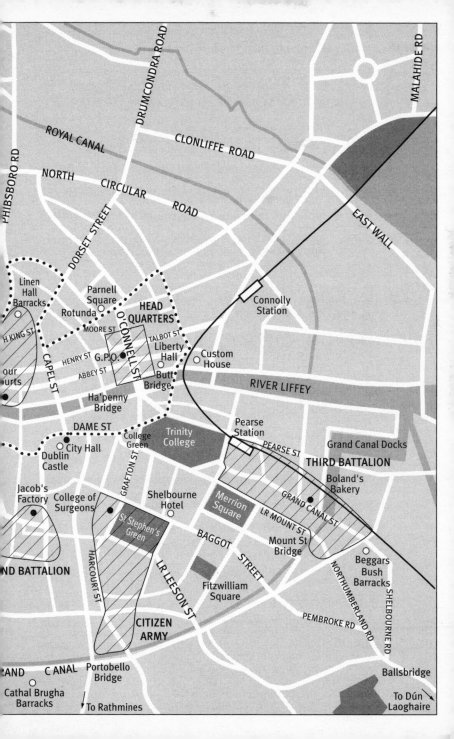

16LIVES – Series Introduction

This book is part of a series called *16 Lives* conceived with the objective of recording for posterity the lives of the sixteen men who were executed after the 1916 Easter Rising. Who were these people and what drove them to commit themselves to violent revolution?

The rank and file as well as the leadership were all from diverse backgrounds. Some were privileged and some had no material wealth. Some were highly educated writers, poets or teachers and others had little formal schooling. Their common desire to set Ireland on the road to national freedom united them under the one banner of the army of the Irish Republic. They occupied key buildings in Dublin and around Ireland for one week before they were forced to surrender. The leaders were singled out for harsh treatment and all sixteen men were executed for their role in the Rising.

The *16 Lives* biographies are meticulously researched yet written in an accessible fashion. Each book can be read as an individual volume but together they make a highly collectable series.

Lorcan Collins & Dr Ruán O'Donnell,
16 Lives *Series Editors*

CONTENTS

Chapter One

• • • • • •

1874 – 1889
Family and Early Life

In the months after the execution of the leaders of the 1916 Rising the *Catholic Bulletin* wrote a series of articles entitled 'Events of Easter Week', describing Michael Mallin as 'Commandant Stephen's Green Command ... a silk weaver and musician, a splendid type of the Dublin tradesman, a credit to the city which cradled him close on forty years ago.'[1] This was very much the conception of Mallin in the years following his execution. A contemporary pamphlet on the leaders of the Rising wrote of Mallin: 'Nor must we forget Michael Mallin ... a silk weaver by profession, a musician and an active temperance advocate, he was one of the most sanguine of all the Company Commanders.'[2]

Of the sixteen men executed for their role in the planning and execution of the rebellion, Michael Mallin is among the lesser known. Virtually nothing has been written about his life before October 1914; he appears in literature about the Rising only after he becomes James Connolly's Chief-of-Staff. Perhaps Michael Mallin has been overshadowed in history by two figures: James Connolly, the only man higher in rank than Mallin in the Irish Citizen Army (ICA), and Countess Constance Markievicz, second-in-command to Mallin during Easter Week 1916. Mallin has almost become 'sandwiched' between these two iconic figures and his own significance neglected as a result.

Michael Thomas Mallin was born into a working-class Dublin family on 1 December 1874 in Ward's Hill in the oldest part of the city, the Liberties. Mallin's eldest son has recorded that he often signed his name as 'M.C. Mallin', the 'C' standing for Christopher and probably a Confirmation name.[3] He was baptised on 6 December in the church of St Nicholas of Myra on Francis Street.

Mallin's father, John, had grown up in the home of his grandfather, also named Michael, at City Quay; his grandfather made parts for sailing ships. John was the son of another John Mallin and Mary Mangan (said to be a daughter or cousin of the poet James Clarence Mangan), and he had a brother, Michael, who died as a young child. John's mother, Mary, disappeared in strange circumstances – she went missing one stormy night and it was thought that a strong wind had swept her into the river Liffey; her body was never found. Soon afterwards, John's father emigrated to Australia, leaving his son with his own father. He was not heard from again and it was rumoured that he was murdered in Australia.

John Mallin had married Sarah Dowling around 1874 and Michael Mallin was born that year. Mallin's mother, who, unlike the rest of the family, was unable to read and write, had worked in a silk factory in Macclesfield, England, but had lost her job when she expressed sympathy for the 'Manchester Martyrs' – in November 1867 William Allen, Michael Larkin and William O'Brien were hanged for their role in an attack on a police van in Manchester in September of that year, an attempt to free two prisoners, during which an unarmed policeman was killed. Sarah Mallin had apparently witnessed the attack on the police van. The execution of the 'Manchester Martyrs' provoked a swell of sympathy for the movement for independence in Ireland. It is not clear if Mallin's mother was sympathetic to the cause prior to events in Manchester (she had family in the British army) or if she was moved by what she had seen, but she does seem to have shown support for the independence movement in later life. Returning to Ireland, she worked in Dublin as a silk winder.

Mallin's mother came from a family steeped in the traditions and culture of the British army, even if she did not share this tendency. Two of her brothers were in the British army, both serving with the Royal Scots Fusiliers. A third, Bartholomew Dowling, had decided to join the priesthood, but instead he met a girl from Connemara on a trip to England and chose to leave his training and get married. At that time it was seen as a source of great shame not to finish one's training as a priest, and that he left to get married only added to the disgrace. To escape this, he decided to sever relations with friends and family and move to America. Having not heard from her brother for a period, Sarah Mallin decided to go to America to find him; she took her young son, Michael, with her. They seem to have stayed in a house in New Bedford, Massachusetts, for a short period until the missing brother was located.[4] Little else is known of this trip.

At the time of Michael's birth in 1874 the family was living in a tenement building at 1 Ward's Hill, the Liberties having the highest concentration of low-value housing in the city. In the 1870s Ward's Hill was characterised by decayed eighteenth-century buildings; fine Georgian houses that had once housed the most affluent members of Dublin's population had been taken over by unscrupulous landlords whose aim was to squeeze every penny of rent possible from these buildings. Whole families occupied single rooms, heating and sanitation was severely lacking and privacy was almost non-existent. At their worst, Dublin's slums were among the most appalling in Europe. Infant mortality was high: of eleven children born to John and Sarah Mallin, six survived to adulthood. Of the surviving children, Michael was the eldest of four brothers, Thomas

(Tom), John and Bartholomew (Bart) and two sisters, Mary (May) and Catherine (Kate or Katie).

Not all who occupied tenement buildings were completely impoverished: in fact, Mallin's father, John Mallin, was a skilled boatwright and carpenter and his father, Michael's grandfather, had a boat-building yard in Dublin, which had been in the family for five generations. The Mallins would have enjoyed a more substantial income than many of those around them, but the poor living conditions made raising a large family difficult.

Mallin's eldest brother, Tom, worked as a carpenter, while brothers John and Bart worked as silk weavers, sisters Mary and Catherine as a biscuit packer and vest maker respectively.[5] According to Tom, Mallin's father was a 'strong nationalist and he and Michael had many a political argument'.[6] Mallin's youngest son, Joseph, has described his own recollections of his father's family:

> Uncle Tom was more outgoing than John or Bart. John's family and his wife were extremely pleasant – no histrionics. ... [aunt] Kate, always seemingly gently amused when talking about the family & others. She was amusing about my grandfather [John Mallin]. He disliked any coarse language and if it started would remark he did not like such talk and would leave the company. [William] Partridge noticed that trait in my father.[7]

The family lived in a number of locations around the Liberties over the years. It was not uncommon for Dublin families at this time to move around the city, often within relatively close proximity, as their financial conditions improved or worsened. In 1889 Mallin's family was living in Marlborough Street and by 1901 they had moved to a residence in Cuffe Street where they would remain for at least the next decade. Little is known about Michael's education but he probably attended the national school in Denmark Street, near the family's home. Like most from his social background, Michael's formal education was brief and basic and he left school in his early teens.

In 1889, shy of his fifteenth birthday, he was persuaded to join the British army by an aunt during a visit to the Curragh in County Kildare. Michael's uncle, James Dowling, had served with the Royal Scots Fusiliers for a number of years in India and was then employed as a Pay Sergeant in the Curragh. Michael seems to have been close to his uncle, often spending summer holidays with him. It was during one of these holidays that Michael first became aware of the Royal Scots Fusiliers. The regiment's band had made a great impression on the young Michael and this is what prompted him to enlist. On hearing that her son had joined the army, Sarah Mallin was worried and angry with him for doing so; he reassured her that it was the musical band that he had joined.[8] Michael Mallin joined the 21st Royal Scots Fusiliers in Birr on 21 October 1889 as a drummer boy, signing up for twelve years' service. Surviving records from his enlistment give a physical description of him as a boy approaching fifteen: he was 4 feet 5 inches in height (he was never to be a tall man), 64lbs with a 'fresh' complexion, grey eyes and brown hair. His regimental number was S.F. 2723.[9]

Chapter Two

1889 – 1902
British Army Career

When Michael Mallin joined the Royal Scots Fusiliers the regiment was on an extended period of home service. Beginning in 1881, fifteen years were spent stationed in Portland (England), Fermoy (County Cork), Birr (County Offaly), Dublin, Glasgow (Scotland) and Aldershot (England). There is little of note for this period in the regimental diary beyond 'annual inspections, and the invariably flattering reports', the Duke of Cambridge apparently declaring that 'such manoeuvring was seldom seen nowadays'.[1] The first battalion, of which Mallin was part, formed a guard for Queen Victoria at Balmoral in 1891.[2]

Following just over eighteen months of 'boy' service, Mallin was given the rank of 'drummer' on 1 June 1891.[3] Traditionally, the role of a drummer in war was to provide a steady beat for the soldiers to march to and to raise troop morale in battle. The rhythm of the drums could also be used by soldiers to keep time when firing or reloading rifles. Though referred to as 'drummers', their duties would often be performed with flutes or bugles. During peacetime the role of the drummer was usually ceremonial: playing at parades, reviews and other events. As part of his training, Mallin learned the flute, violin, studied music theory and obtained a 3rd class certification on 13 March 1893.[4] Aside from their musical requirements, band members also received much of the same basic training as regular members of the infantry. In 1894 Mallin earned the grade of 'marksman' for the first time and was to obtain this grade – first class or second class marksman – each year until his discharge.[5]

Mallin seems to have been a disciplined soldier. Although he was never promoted beyond the grade of drummer, he earned increases through 'Good Conduct Pay' on three occasions throughout his service: 1d (one penny) following two years' service in 1891; 2d following six years' service in 1895; 3d following twelve in 1901.[6] He was also, apparently, a useful lightweight boxer and won a couple of medals for sport.[7]

In 1896 the Royal Scots Fusiliers were sent to India, then part of the British empire, and Mallin began what amounted to a stay of over six years there on 24 September. For the first eight months the regiment occupied various stations in the Punjab, north India. As noted by John Buchan, who published a history of the regiment in 1925, at this point the Scots Fusiliers were 'very near to active service, for the mutterings of trouble were beginning in the frontier hills.' Mallin's first, and only, period of active service followed: the 'Tirah campaign', often referred to in contemporary accounts as the 'Tirah expedition'. This campaign lasted about two years and consisted of a series of encounters with various native tribes.

The Tirah region is in modern-day Pakistan, but in the nineteenth century was part of British India. Trouble first erupted in the Khyber Pass, a mountain pass leading to Afghanistan, which formed a significant part of the lucrative 'Silk Road' trade route. From the early 1880s the Afridi (a collection of Indian tribes) had guarded the Khyber Pass in return for a subsidy from the British India Government. The government had formed a number of defensive posts in the area manned by units of Afridi. In July and August 1897 there was a general uprising of these tribes. In his work on the regiment, John Buchan linked this uprising to the 'wide resurgence of Moslem pride which followed Turkey's easy victory over Greece.' The Afridi destroyed the posts guarded by their own countrymen along the Khyber Pass. Meanwhile, in the Swat and Tochi valleys to the north-east of the pass, the Mohmand tribe had risen against the British. By October, the Mohmands had been suppressed by two British divisions moving from Makaland and Pashawur respectively, with the loss of nearly a quarter of the force. Then the Afridi tribes attacked the British forts at Samana Range, further south. Sir William Lockhart was tasked with assembling the Tirah Expeditionary Force to deal with this more troubling outbreak. The native tribes used their knowledge of the landscape to inflict an often devastating guerrilla campaign on the regular troops. John Buchan has described some of the difficulties facing the army in quelling the local tribes:

> Between them the Afridis and the Orakzais could bring more than 40,000 men into the field – men armed not with jezails and old muzzle-loaders, but with [more modern and efficient] Martini-Henrys or stolen Lee-Metfords. The terrain, too, was most intricate and difficult – one of which Wellington's words in the Pensinsula were true: 'If you make war in that country with a large army, you starve; and if you go into it with a small one, you get beaten.'[8]

By December 1899, however, the local tribes had been sufficiently suppressed to end 'this sharp little campaign'.[9] Mallin was awarded with the India medal (1895), with the 'Punjab frontier' clasp (1897-98) and the 'Tirah' clasp (1897-98).[10] Following the end of the Tirah campaign, the Royal Scots Fusiliers remained in India, stationed in various towns and cities in the north of the country (including Landi Khotal, Peshawur, Cherat, Chakrata, Allahabad, Bareilly, Amritsar and Jubbulpore) with no 'break in the monotony of its life.'[11]

Although the British Army was still active in India the Scots Fusiliers were not called into action.

While on leave in Ireland, some time before leaving for India, Mallin joined a friend of the Hickey family in visiting their home, between Lucan and Chapelizod in Dublin. There he met Patrick Hickey's young daughter, Agnes. Mr Hickey was originally far from happy to have a British soldier visiting his house. He was an old Fenian and had been exiled for his role in the 1867 uprising. Soon, however, they became close friends. From the end of 1894 until his return from India in 1902, Mallin kept up a regular correspondence with Agnes, and they became engaged to be married. Letters that Mallin wrote have survived and offer a rare and tantalising glimpse of Mallin's time in India, his attitudes to the war he was asked to fight and the flag under which he fought.[12] He writes in an unpunctuated, continuous-flow style, with regular misspellings.

For most of the 'Tirah campaign' (1897-98) Mallin was stationed in Sialkot. He seems to have made little reference to his orders or the fighting itself in his correspondence with Agnes, except in one early letter, sent from Sialkot in November 1897, in which he gave a detailed description of a battle at the Ublan Pass, just outside Kohat in modern-day Pakistan. Mallin was part of a force that was given orders to 'clear the enemy off the hills about six miles away'. He mentions that he was with 'H' company as they were short of buglers, suggesting that he fulfilled the traditional role of a drummer or bugler during the fighting. This is the only mention of his own duties in the field in the letters. He had some infantry training, including in musketry, but it is not clear if he ever fired a rifle in battle. For this engagement the men set off at three thirty in the morning with only 'a pint of tea one gill of rum in it and one biscute [sic] we had to march six miles and fight on that.' They spent much of the time walking in 'the bed of a river ... the water was past [sic] our knees very near the whole time.' Mallin described the scene when they reached the enemy:

> the Artillery set the ball rolling you should have heard the shouting of the enemy as soon as the shells burst amongst them as soon as the Artillery had done with them we moved to the attack the enemy rolling big stones on top of us one of them struck two native soldiers killed one and broke the other poor fellows [sic] legs.

Three of the native soldiers were killed and five wounded. They reached the top of the hill, but the enemy had moved to another hill and showered them with bullets, forcing a retreat. However, when they retired from the hill, the enemy 'swarmed up it again' and they had to fight again. This time the artillery could not be used as the soldiers were too near the target. Mallin related how:

> we started to loose [sic] the men the first to fall was a man

of ours ... shot through the head and two shots in his body one Officer of the native Infantry and two men killed then we lost annother [sic] man killed and two Officers severely wounded and four men slightly [wounded].

Mallin reports that this engagement happened about three o'clock, nearly twelve hours after they had set out and the men had had nothing to eat and their water was all gone: 'our men were calling for water my tongue was swollen in my mouth one of our men went mad.' They were saved by the native soldiers in the British army who offered their own water as 'they could stand the heat better' and could last without it. Fourteen hours after they left – fourteen hours since they had eaten – the men returned to camp. Mallin had been very slightly wounded when a bullet hit a rock beside him and a shard of rock hit him in the neck.[13]

After the battle at Ublan Pass, Mallin contracted a serious case of malaria. He wrote to Agnes that when they returned the men were forced to sleep outside their tents in their clothes 'in case of a night attack'. This is, apparently, how he caught the malaria. Mallin downplayed it as a 'slight attack' that had 'given him a bit of a shake' but also mentioned that he had lost two and a half stone in weight during his illness.[14] During the rest of his stay in India he suffered occasional attacks of the symptoms and more time in hospital. In a letter to Agnes written in November 1900, Mallin described a particularly uncomfortable period in hospital:

I was lying in hospital when your loving letter came to me last week and I could not write. This is the worst attack I have had in the country I have remitting fever and a touch of ague [periods of chills, fever and sweating] this is my tenth day in and I am nearly out of my mind drinking great doses of queenine [sic] not in little spoonful's that you Nurses [Agnes worked as a nurse] are good enough to give but a wine glass full three times a day oh it is horrid stuff.[15]

Symptoms of the malaria would sporadically appear for the rest of his life.[16]

Mallin had thought that his illness might prevent him from returning to the front and he wrote to Agnes: 'I may have to go back to the front but I dont [sic] think so. if I do I shall let you know.' On 19 December 1897, less than a month after leaving hospital, he sent 'Just a few lines to let you know I have to go to the front at once we have lost a lot of men this last few days ... We have to take the Kiber Pass [sic] on the 22nd we have two days on the train and one days [sic] march through the enemy country.'[17] Later, from Cherat in 1899 when the Tirah campaign was over, he gave a rare and revealing account of a time when he had been in significant danger during the campaign:

One night when my company was lost in the dark up in the last expedition and the enemy were yelling like mad men round us after what seemed [like] ages the Captain said men it is every one for himself good by [sic] men in case I never get in just then he was shot down I thought to myself will Agnes pray for me or is she praying for me we lost five men and a[n] officer that night we never saw four of out of [sic] the five poor fellows since you must always pray for me my darling.[18]

Away from the danger of the battlefield, Mallin had a number of narrow escapes. He related one remarkable tale to Agnes in March 1897:

I had quite a little adventure the Dr[u]ms went out on a paper chase [a game where a designated 'hare' sets off and is followed by 'hounds' who follow a trail of paper left by the 'hare'] on horses we started off at nine am I was one of the hares the other one was a Lt Corpral [sic] and he knew the country very well but we went a little off the track and were lost for some hours and where did we finde [sic] ourselves but in the woods of the Rajha [Raja – an Indian prince] of Jumus Domine the natives about there do not like us very much of course a crowd of them got around us and started beating us with sticks we would never [have] got away from them if it had not been for a dog that we had with us. Natives are very frightened of dogs at least our dogs because soldiers train them to hate natives.[19]

One night in March 1902 in Chakrata, Mallin had another run in with some natives and believed that 'only I was in

Dr[u]ms I would most likely have been thrown down the Kuds, however I am safe in my room.' Though it is unclear what he meant by 'the Kuds', there is an implication here that army musicians were viewed differently to other soldiers by the rebels and were, perhaps, in less danger of the kind of attack Mallin mentioned.

After the Tirah campaign had officially ended in December 1899, Mallin's regiment was not again involved in combat. As will be seen, Mallin developed a strong distaste for the army and the war in India but a comment made from Allahabad in June 1901 indicates that Mallin had enjoyed the excitement and danger of life at the front, or at least found it preferable to some of the more mundane aspects of regular life in India:

I would like to be back on the Frontier the danger of having your head blown off made it nice and exciting here it is to[o] safe and easy.[20]

Previously, in 1898 he had written:

I cannot be in very bad health doing all those things but I am recommended for the hills on account of my health in the Tirah Campaign weather [sic] I shall go up or not I cannot say yet I hope I do go it will do me good.[21]

He does, however, seem to have experienced some joy from his musical duties. In April 1901, he wrote:

I am hard at work at the present time what with Playing at Dances Regimental Concerts & Theatre I have my work cut out I can assure [you] but I don't mind the work love it is a pleasure to me I can Play the Flute very well a little of the Violin, Mandolin & Banjo I have been asked to get up a Mandoline [sic] and Banjo band in the Regiment.[22]

He also continued his musketry practice. In 1898 he informed Agnes he was 'the best shot in the company again this year (score 173) that makes it three times out of four the first prise [sic] is £1.18.6. and the honour of being best shot'; and in 1901, 'I have proved myself the best shot in my company and wear gold guns and a star on my arm.'[23]

One remarkable story has emerged from Mallin's time in India and though there is little supporting evidence, it is worth relating. It seems that Mallin often told the story himself and this is how it has survived. As the tale goes, a British officer was shot by an Indian nationalist at a British army event. Mallin had witnessed the shooting and was able to identify the shooter. A native man was arrested and tried. Fourteen witnesses were called to the stand and of the fourteen, Mallin was the only one to maintain that the accused was innocent. The man was, nevertheless, convicted and executed on the basis of the evidence of the other thirteen witnesses. It is then claimed that local Indian nationalists took their revenge on those who had given evidence at the trial and only Mallin escaped unharmed.[24] Though the details of these events are impossible to clarify, it seems that the shooting and subsequent trial and execution did actually take place. It is an important part of Mallin's development as it shows sympathy towards local nationalists in India, and also an acute sense of justice and honesty. It may have also been a pivotal event in the growth of Mallin's anti-imperial beliefs, which will be described later.

As well as writing to Agnes Hickey, Mallin appears to have kept a regular correspondence with Agnes's mother and her sister, Josephine, during his stay in India. Two letters to his soon to be mother-in-law have survived. Mallin developed a close relationship with Mrs Hickey, and there is evidence of genuine warmth in the surviving letters. He refers to her affectionately as 'Dear mother' in one and signs off as 'Your affectionate future son'. Writing from Allahabad on 25 May 1901 Mallin consoled Mrs Hickey on the death of her husband ('you must not let your-self run down in spirits now about your Mr Hickey he is in a better place than us please God') and passed on optimistic thoughts ('we always have something to live for and I dont think we will always be in the same condition that we are now').[25]

Mallin's twelve years of service was due to expire on 21 October 1901, just over a month short of his twenty-seventh birthday. In a letter to Agnes in June 1899 he declared, 'I come home in October 1901', and just over a year later, 'yes dear it will not be long till I am home'.[26] He was, however, required to remain in India. By May 1901 Mallin was aware that he might be kept over time. Writing to Mrs Hickey, he noted: 'I dont know what I will do if I am kept over my time but when the boats does start [sic] I am one of the first to get a passage. I may have to do a few months extra if the War is not finished.'[27] Three days before he was officially due to be discharged Mallin was certain he would have to stay and wrote to Agnes pointing out that the army had ordered that all long-service men must be discharged three months before they reach thirteen years, and 'well dear I shall have twelve years and nine months service next July'.[28] He was still in Allahabad in September, but informed Agnes that one boat was leaving on 17 September and another on 25 September and 'I am sure to get one of those I expect the first.' On 10 September he wrote to say that he would, in fact, be leaving on 19 September only to be informed two days later that it would be the next month before he could get a boat.[29]

Almost a full year after he was due for discharge (October 1902) Mallin again wrote to Mrs Hickey from India: 'am waiting patiently for the order to proceed home it will not be long now a matter of weeks that is all'. Aggrieved by the delay but clearly aware of the futility of complaint he added, 'even then the government has broken it [sic] contract with me I will have thirteen years and five or six weeks and you know that is not fair atal [sic] well we must put up with it and not grumble'.[30] Mallin's final weeks of service in India consisted of further delay, frustration and illness. Mallin was again hospitalised, probably with another attack of malaria, as he wrote to Agnes on 31 October, 'my Coleen Dass [sic], I am still in hospital but well and strong again'. He reported that in a week's time he was to travel from Allahabad to the transit camp at Deolali, a three-day journey, before waiting ten days there to catch the boat home.[31] From his next letter, of 13 November 1902, it seems that his illness had meant that he was sent as an invalid to catch an earlier boat only to find that he had arrived too late, the boat was full and he would have to wait until 22 November. Even then, there was another frustrating delay and the boat did not leave until 25 November. In his final letter to Agnes from India he wrote, 'I will arrive in Gosport [England] on the 16th of next month [December] ... this is the last letter to write to you from India, I will be home a few days after it myself'.[32] Two days of 'home' service followed before Mallin was finally discharged on 18 December 1902. He had just turned twenty-eight. His service totalled thirteen years and fifty-nine days.[33]

Thomas Mallin has stated that his brother was asked to remain in the army as a band sergeant but refused, telling his adjutant 'he wanted to go home as he wanted to forget that he was ever a soldier.'[34] Perhaps Mallin simply wished to forget that he was a British soldier, as this statement, written nearly fifty years after the event, is certainly at odds with the path Mallin was to follow in civilian life.

Legacy

Extracts from Mallin's letters to Agnes Hickey from 1898 to 1901 reveal some important developments in Mallin's ideology and politics in his early twenties. Mallin's political beliefs radicalised during his time in India and he grew to detest having to serve with the British army. In one letter he revealed to Agnes that 'the British army is a Hell on earth I wish I were well out of it but I did not think it was so bad until I came out here'.[35] Mallin felt this way as he had come to disagree with the aims of the war that he and the British army were fighting in India and his sympathies lay with the native rebels. He pointed out in another letter:

> the war is lasting a very long time dear we aught [sic] to leave the poor people alone for I am sure they will never give in and they have proved brave men God help them if I were not a soldier I would be out fighting for them.[36]

He goes further on another occasion and writes, 'I wish it was for Erin that I was fighting and not against these poor people'.[37] Mallin repeats this desire to fight for Ireland against British rule a number of times. After he received his medal for the Tirah campaign, Mallin contrasted his pride at his military achievement with the cause for which he earned it: 'I am very proud dear to have a medal but would be far prouder if it was for Ireland I earned it'. He also acknowledged the role played by the British army in Ireland, adding, 'it is the likes of me that keeps mine and your country down God help her.'[38] In 1901, when Mallin knew he would no longer be required to take part in active service, he presciently commented, 'all the chance of being killed fighting for the robber flag that I am serving under is all over if ever I am to die by bayonet or bullet I hope it is against it for Ireland'.[39]

For Mallin, there was a clear link between social and religious injustice in Ireland (and, indeed, in India) and British rule. In a letter of September 1898 he explained to Agnes that 'it made the Irish men very bitter out here while we are fiting [sic] for England's Queen and Government they were letting our poor people starve'.[40] Mallin also makes a scathing remark about Irish MPs, responsible for representing Ireland at the British Parliament in Westminster:

> In poor Ireland God save her she is in a bad state is there no good and true men to lift her up and strike out for her strong and hard if I had my way I would take all our members of parliament out into the Bay put a rope round their necks with a stone at the end of it and throw them in they are only using the poor people for their own ends.[41]

This suggests that Mallin had little or no faith that the politicians of the day would solve the plight of the poor in Ireland. Agnes sent Irish newspapers and kept him informed about events in Ireland and this seems to have had an important influence on his attitude towards British imperialism and the army. In September 1898 he notes that he:

> read somethings [sic] which is not fit for me to mention in
> the paper that makes my blood boil to think of it. If the Sol-
> dierery (sic) done half what is said of them they are burning
> in Hell as sure as there is a good God in heaven'

before passionately adding:

> a day will come when we will be able to pay England back
> with Interest all she has done to us and I hope I am alive
> and in Ireland I will help to pay it.

It is not clear what event Mallin was referring to, and it
may not have even taken place in Ireland, but his heated
response is noteworthy. Mallin also refers to a large demonstration in Dublin that Agnes had described for him, most
likely an event to commemorate the centenary of the 1798
rebellion:

> it must have been a splendid sight but how much grander it
> would have been if it had been a demonstration to selebrate
> [sic] our Independance [sic] but God is good and it will
> come to pass yet Dear Agnes.[42]

From the many references to God in the letters, it is clear
that Mallin's faith was deeply important to him. The attitude
of the Protestant British monarch and state towards Catholicism had a definite impact on his growing hatred for the

British empire. Queen Victoria, who also held the title of Empress of India, died in January 1901. In May 1901 Mallin informed Agnes that he had 'refused to give a subscription to the Queen's Memorial until the Oath is changed but here I am a soldier making threats'[43] – on coronation, the British monarch was required to swear an oath to uphold the Protestant faith in Britain, and Mallin would not contribute money towards a memorial for Queen Victoria for this reason. His brother, Thomas, suggested later that this was one of a number of similar incidents that prevented Mallin from obtaining a higher commission in the army.[44] Queen Victoria was succeeded by her son, Edward VII. Having read an article sent to him by Agnes, Mallin was incensed at a comment or comments made by Edward VII in April 1901 and wrote:

> is it not terrible are we to allow even a king to say such things of us and our Religion I only hope the day will come when I for one will be able to pay them back for all the insults and I think there are thousands who will so as I would if there was only a chance, I would not say all this to you my love only I know you are a true daughter of Ireland and our holy Church my darling you do not know what we Irish-men and Catholics have to put up with in the Army.[45]

On 30 July 1902 Mallin joined the Confraternity of the Lady of Our Sacred Heart. Soon afterwards, on his return to Dublin, he joined the Workingmen's Temperance Society, which had been founded by Capuchin priests in the city.[46]

In later life, Mallin did not deny or downplay his British army career and it was widely known that he had been a British soldier. Liam Ó Briain, who fought under Mallin in 1916, learned from another source that Mallin had been a British soldier and that 'he had done the Chitral campaign, 1896, [sic] but not, he was proud to say, the Boer War.'[47] A second battalion of the Royal Scots Fusiliers, founded in 1858, had been sent from India to South Africa to deal with the Boer uprising. There was much nationalist support in Ireland for the Boer cause and Mallin was clearly keen to make this distinction.

There is clear evidence in Michael Mallin's letters to Agnes Hickey that he became radicalised during his British army service in India. The social injustice and inequality that Mallin read about and witnessed first-hand convinced him that Ireland must rid itself of British rule. It becomes obvious that Mallin believed, even as early as 1898, that physical force was necessary to achieve this and that he hoped to play his part and use his British army training and experience against the British. This, however, did not happen immediately. There were several steps in between. Given the concern with the poor and social issues in Ireland evident at times in his letters, it is not surprising that the next great step on Mallin's path to rebellion in 1916 was into trade unionism and socialism in Dublin.

Chapter Three

1903 – 1913
Silk Weaver and Musician;
Trade Unionist and Socialist

On 26 April 1903, Michael Mallin married Agnes Hickey in Chapelizod Church.[1] Agnes was born around 1875, the daughter of Patrick and Mary Hickey. Agnes Hickey's family lived in Hibernian Terrace in Chapelizod and were reasonably well off; she worked as a nurse and her father and brother were tailors. Her father, Patrick Hickey, had been exiled for eleven years for his role in the 1867 Fenian Rising and her grandfather was also an active nationalist.[2] Agnes had an older brother, Patrick, and two sisters, Josephine and Jane.

When he and Agnes married, Mallin was living with his family in a tenement building at 12 Cuffe Street. They then spent four years in a small house in Wellington Street. Their first son, James, was born on 21 February 1904. A second son, John, was born there in 1906. In later life both James and John were known by their Irish names, Séamus and Seán, although it is not clear if this was the case during their father's lifetime; their names are listed in English on the family's 1911 census return. Not untypical of Dublin families at the time, the family moved regularly around the city between 1908 and 1909, probably the result of fluctuating financial circumstances. In 1908 they spent a brief period in Blessington Street, before opening a shop at 111 Capel Street. Soon after, they opened another shop in a small, red-brick house at 40 Hamilton Street. Their first daughter, Una, was born in Hamilton Street in 1908. By 1910 Michael and Agnes Mallin were living in a house at 65 Meath Street, on a site recently converted from a tenement building, running another small shop selling tobacco and newspapers, where they remained for a number of years. Another son, Joseph, was born in 1914.[3]

On the certificate for their marriage, Michael's occupation is listed as case-maker. Mallin may have secured this work through his father who was working as a carpenter. It was a short-lived career, however, as soon afterwards he began to work as a silk weaver in Messrs Richard Atkinson and Company, poplin manufacturers. Mallin had the right to work as a weaver as his maternal family were weavers.[4] Weaving was a trade that was traditionally passed down through families; those who did not have family connections in the industry were not welcome. It is not clear if Mallin served the usual apprenticeship with Atkinson's. He seems to have learned to weave – and may even have served some kind of apprenticeship – while in the British army and was, therefore, entitled to work as a journeyman weaver. His son, Séamus, has speculated as much.[5] Séamus recalls that his father was quite skilled and often took him to the factory to watch him and his colleagues at work.[6]

Silk weaving was a revitalised industry (for a period at least) in Dublin when Mallin became a weaver. The Liberties, where Mallin grew up, was the traditional base of silk weaving in the city. It was long claimed that it was Huguenot refugees, fleeing persecution in France in the seventeenth century, who established the weaving industry in the Liberties. While Huguenot settlers did contribute to a revitalisation of weaving in the city, it is now clear that a weaver's guild had been established in Dublin as far back as 1446.[7] Poplin was introduced in Dublin shortly after the establishment of the silk weaving industry. Poplin, a combination of silk and wool woven together to produce a silk-faced fabric with the strength and durability of wool, became a popular and successful textile in Dublin soon after its introduction. The term 'Irish poplin' is used to describe the type of fabric woven by skilled weavers in Dublin; to be given the title, the fabric must be composed of pure silk and wool and woven, by hand, in Ireland. To use the term Irish poplin to describe any material not produced in this way is illegal. By the late nineteenth century, however, the formerly booming poplin industry was in decline. In 1890 there were only twenty looms working in the Liberties. At the turn of the century, however, the poplin tie became fashionable and it is this single item that resulted in a new lease of life for the industry; by 1903 the number of working looms in the city increased to one hundred and seventeen, and by 1911 this number was one hundred and ninety-three.[8] It was into this newly invigorated industry that Mallin entered.

Messrs Richard Atkinson and Company was one of four old, established firms in poplin weaving in Dublin, the other three being Elliot and Son, Messrs Pim Brothers and Messrs Fry and Company. Atkinson's was founded in 1820 by Alderman Richard Atkinson, who was twice Lord Mayor of Dublin. When Atkinson founded his company, weaving was done on looms built in the weavers' own homes. Workers supplied the goods for Atkinson's shop on College Green. The materials were collected from the manufacturer, taken to the weaver's house, where it was then woven, and the finished cloth was brought back for sale. Richard Atkinson is remembered for visiting his weavers on horseback and for insisting on strict discipline and high-quality workmanship.[9] Apprenticeships could only be taken up by the son of a weaver or by someone from a weaving family. Following the medieval tradition of apprenticeships, apprentices were indentured to journeyman (qualified) weavers. As there were no factories the apprentice was sent to live with his master as one of his family for the duration of his education. Silk weavers were paid not by the hour, but by the number of yards of material they produced in a week. To compensate the master for time lost in teaching his apprentice, he received half of the apprentice's earnings. After three years, the apprentice was trained well enough to produce his own work. He would then receive two thirds of what he earned from this work. This amount was increased during the fifth year and by the final year the apprentice received eleven pence out of every shilling. Having qualified, he had to leave and find work in another city or country (hence the term 'journeyman') or build a loom in his own home and work from there.

It was only in the early twentieth century that silk weaving factories came into existence. Atkinson's had a factory and shop in College Green, Dublin and another factory in Hanbury Lane, where Mallin was employed. The creation of factories meant an end to much of the home weaving, but some weavers also continued to use looms at home. Working in factories, weavers were still paid only for what they produced. Any time spent waiting at the looms for material to arrive was time during which the weaver could not earn. In addition, weavers had to pay their employer or manufacturer a 'loom rent' of one shilling per week for the use of their loom. Padraig Breathnach, a silk weaver in Dublin for over seventy years, recalls that in 1903 he was earning an average of twenty-two or twenty-three shillings a week (a general labourer would have got about eighteen shillings a week). At the time Breathnach became an apprentice, the master of the indentured weaver had to pay the secretary of the trade one shilling a week, as well as the loom rent. At the end of the week the weaver was able to draw the amount of money he believed his work had earned. However, the weaver could often draw more than he had earned for the week simply by filling in a docket. The deficit was recorded as a debt to the employer, meaning the weaver was continually going into debt. Breathnach has noted the benefits of this system for the employer:

> One employer told me the debt system was a good invest-
> ment. The employee couldn't, according to the rules of the
> trade and according to the law of the land too, he couldn't
> leave that employer without first paying the debt. He'd have
> to come back and work for him. He had a hold on him, he
> couldn't go.

This practice changed, claims Breathnach, after the arrival of James Larkin.[10]

Trade unionism in Ireland had flagged severely in the late 1890s, but was regenerated by the arrival of James Larkin to Belfast in 1907 where he led a strike of Belfast dock workers. The strength and militancy of the union movement was further enhanced by Larkin's establishment of the Irish Transport and General Workers' Union (ITGWU) in Dublin in 1909. Silk weavers had their own union which may have been founded was early as 1680. Board of Trade records give the number of members of the Dublin Silk and Poplin Weaver's Trade Union each year from 1892 to 1910 but no other details are given. Between 1892 and 1901 membership ranged between fifty-four and eighty members. In 1902 membership was ninety-two and it rose steadily each year to a peak of 320 in 1909, reflecting renewed prosperity in the industry after the turn of the century. There are, unfortunately, no surviving detailed records of the union or its activities. The union was reorganised in 1918 as the Dublin Silk Trade Society, but was dissolved in December 1936.[11]

An indenture allowing Bartholomew Mallin to become an apprentice silk weaver with Michael Downey, co-signed 'Secretary M. Mallin' and dated 23 August 1908, survives in the Allen Library's collection.[12] An earlier indenture signed by Mallin, dated 8 July, apprenticing Edward Gibson to Mr N. Alexander (both of whom took part in the rebellion in 1916) was presented to the National Museum in 1935.[13] This indicates that as early as 1908 Mallin had become secretary of the Silk Weaver's Trade Union. The lack of any records or papers for the Silk Weavers' Union makes it impossible to ascertain a specific date, but Mallin was certainly in the role by July 1908.

On 31 October 1906 Messrs McBirney poplin manufactures were summoned to court by Michael Harbourne, chairman of the Silk Weavers' Union, for a false trade description. McBirney's were accused of selling neckties manufactured in Britain as 'Irish poplin'. Dublin poplin manufacturers had grown suspicious of items sold in McBirney's and determined to investigate further. On 20 August, Harbourne, Mallin and another weaver purchased a tie labelled 'Irish poplin'. Mallin requested a guarantee that the tie was made in Ireland and an invoice was produced. Those called as witnesses, including Mallin and the manager of Atkinson's, R.S. Swirles, confirmed that the tie was not Irish poplin. The court case made the front page in the *Evening Herald* and was reported in the *Evening Mail* (notable for a large McBirney's advertisement on a previous page) and *Evening Telegraph* as well as the national *Irish Times*. T.M. Healy, a well-known nationalist MP, represented the British firm who sold the material to McBirney's.[14] The case shows the Dublin silk trade's insistence on the authenticity of Irish poplin and the steps taken to prosecute counterfeits. Each weaver called could tell Irish poplin from a fake simply by its appearance and texture, highlighting the skilled nature of the industry. This case is also the earliest recorded example of Mallin's participation in the affairs of the Silk Weavers' Union.

His appointment as secretary to the union around 1908 represents Mallin's first official trade union position and is a post he held until 1914. That he was to become secretary of the union within five years of taking up employment in the industry is significant. That he was willing to take on the role so soon into his career is, perhaps, more telling. Further, this was a substantial extra commitment for a man with a very young family. It is impossible to assess his effectiveness in the position, but, as mentioned above, there was a sharp increase in the number of members between 1906 and 1910 and by the time the factory's weavers went on strike in 1913 it seems the majority of workers in Messrs Atkinson were members.

How influential Mallin was in the resurgence of the union or whether it was simply a natural progression for a trade experiencing a boom is, again, impossible to judge. Around 1910, during Mallin's time as secretary, a new Weavers' Hall was built in Donore Avenue. Prior to this, meetings had been held in local public houses, where rooms were given free of charge as an inevitable round of drinks followed each meeting. Teenage apprentices were often indentured at these meetings. As trade was good at this time and the number of apprentices increasing, it was decided to build the hall to keep these impressionable teenagers away from the influence of the public houses, something Mallin, a temperance advocate, would have favoured.[15] There is little other evidence of Mallin's day-to-day role as secretary, one incident aside. In July 1911 a letter appeared in the *Irish Times* signed by then chairman of the Silk Weavers' Union, John Maloney, and Mallin. The letter was a copy of one sent to the private secretary of the queen. During the royal visit that year the queen had worn Irish poplin on her entrance to Dublin. The society wished to thank her for her selection and her 'interest in their historic industry.'[16]

Beyond the weaver's union, Mallin was engaged in other work that offers a significant insight into his interests and ambitions at this time. James O'Shea, a neighbour who would later fight under Mallin during the Rising, claims that, in 1909, Mallin organised a small boy scouts group to rival the British or Baden Powell Scout movement. According to O'Shea, the group contained around twelve boys and was run from his small shop in Capel Street. Mallin often took the group to the Dublin mountains on Sundays to train. Mallin's brother, Thomas, also mentions a boy's group run by Mallin from Capel Street in his statement to the Bureau of Military History.[17] In his book, *The History of the Irish Citizen Army*, first published in 1943, R.M. Fox states that 'This scout movement was the forerunner of the Fianna Éireann formed by Madame Markievicz a little later.'[18] Diarmuid Lynch has expressed scepticism about this comment in his own book, *The IRB and the 1916 Insurrection*, published over a decade later. Lynch believes there is no 'analogy' between Mallin's group and Fianna Éireann. Lynch is doubtful about Mallin's involvement in the nationalist movement in 1909 (though reluctantly so) as well as his early connections with Markievicz, adding, 'Mallin had been, I believe, a British soldier and mighty few ex-soldiers would touch any kind of *national* movement prior to the establishment of the Irish Volunteers in 1913'.[19] Lynch is certainly correct to question Fox's statement: Mallin's scouts were a small and seemingly short-lived group, and to describe it as a 'movement' is to exaggerate their size somewhat. It is also not entirely unlikely that there was some mistrust of Mallin in certain nationalist circles and within the scouting movement in 1909, due to his British army background. Comments by James O'Shea testify to this. O'Shea claims Mallin had contacted the Fianna leadership 'and was turned down immediately by the powers as he was an ex-soldier' and 'got a bad time of it when he spoke on scouting at its initial meeting from a guy who did not turn out in 1916.' Interestingly, O'Shea believes that one of the 'powers' to turn Mallin away was Countess Markievicz.[20] If this was the case, it is worth noting given their future role together and again serves to discredit Fox's statement. Conversely, O'Shea was one of the Citizen Army members who contributed information to Fox and it is almost certainly from O'Shea that Fox gleaned his information on the scout group.

Regardless, this small group is more significant for what it tells us about Mallin's own interests. Groups such as Mallin's and its larger counterparts around the country are symptomatic of a growing level of militarism in Ireland and an increased interest in military-style training and the health and moral benefits of such training. Mallin clearly retained an interest in this type of activity and the scout group was likely his first involvement in training and organising after his discharge from the British army. If the Fianna had, in fact, rejected Mallin initially, it does not seem to have affected his enthusiasm for this activity.

A new Socialist Party of Ireland was established in 1904, an amalgamation of the Irish Socialist Republican Party (ISRP) and the Socialist Labour Party. The Irish Socialist Republican Party was founded by James Connolly in 1903 (and once unkindly said to have more syllables than members). Following a split in the party and Connolly's departure for America in 1903, the party collapsed. One side of the split founded the Socialist Labour Party, but by 1904 they had re-amalgamated to form the Socialist Party of Ireland. By 1909 divisions had arisen in the Socialist Party of Ireland and a socialist unity conference was convened by labour leader and organiser William O'Brien, following writings by James Connolly in *The Nation* newspaper.

The conference took place on 13 June in the Trades Hall, Capel Street, chaired by O'Brien and attended by 150 people. One of the key results of the unity conference was a re-launch of the Socialist Party of Ireland. A unity committee was also established onto which Mallin was elected.

Other elected members included O'Brien, his brother Daniel, and pacifist and future founder member of the Irish Citizen Army, Francis Sheehy-Skeffington. Some of the policy measures agreed upon by this committee included pressing for independent labour representation on elected bodies, support for the national language and for democratic discussion to take place on the means of advancing socialism in Ireland.[21] While the weaver's union marks Mallin's interest in trade unionism, this appointment to the socialist unity committee places Mallin firmly among the leading Dublin socialists at the time.

Michael Mallin is often described as a 'silk weaver and musician', particularly in contemporary accounts after his death.[22] Music was to play a prominent role in Mallin's life from the time he joined the Royal Scots Fusiliers. He became proficient in a number of other musical instruments, most notably the flute. Having left the army, Mallin showed a particular flair for conducting fife and drum bands. He developed a reputation as an impressive conductor, winning numerous medals and trophies.[23] Mallin conducted the City of Dublin Fife and Drum Band between 1913 and 1914. The band played concerts in St Michan's Park, Halston Street, in each of these years.[24] He also conducted a band founded by a Leon Federston which performed in Dublin and around the country. The most well known photograph of Mallin, later used on commemorative postcards and in literature, is taken from the programme of a concert given by the band in the Antient Concert Rooms in Dublin. He also acted in at least one play, a piece written by Constance Markievicz.[25] Later, Mallin took charge of the Emmet Fife and Drum Band, based in the Emmet Hall in Inchicore. It is likely that his involvement with this band led him to become a member of the Irish Transport and General Workers' Union.

While Chief-of-Staff of the Irish Citizen Army, Mallin conducted the four-piece Worker's Orchestra. They played on Sunday nights in Liberty Hall.[26] James O'Shea and Frank Robbins have noted how Mallin would play the flute as the men sang songs on their return from route marches and excursions. On the evening before the outbreak of the Easter Rising in 1916, Easter Sunday, the ICA held their usual recital. Michael Mallin played the flute and Maeve Cavanagh played piano.[27] Two flutes, believed to have belonged to Mallin, are now in the possession of the Kilmainham Gaol museum.

Mallin was able to supplement his weaving income by teaching music to local children. Students came to the family home in Wellington Street to learn the violin and he also gave lessons to groups. Séamus Mallin remembered his own violin lessons, but remarked that what he most enjoyed was when his father would play a piece by Bach for him: 'I cannot say if he played it well but I was under his spell.' Music was not always profitable, however. A number of Mallin's musical concerts, including those in the Antient Concert Rooms, suffered a loss but Mallin persevered.[28] As will be seen later, they were among a number of unsuccessful endeavours.

Mallin lived a relatively quiet and happy life in Meath Street. Séamus Mallin has described those years:

> Although there were big changes in life coming in the following years we did not know it yet. The years between 1910 and 1913 were the most valuable they [his parents] had. We often went on holidays to Skerries or the Isle of Man. During the holidays it was a habit of my father to read out loud to my mother, something she really loved. Needless to say there was nothing to stop us listening also. It was history that he was most interested in, mainly the history of South America. He also loved Ancient Europe and I knew about Hannibal and the Romans before I ever knew there were countries called Germany and France there at all. As for novels, he preferred the ones written by Joseph Conrad.[29]

This quiet period came to an end in March 1913, when Mallin's union went on strike.

Chapter Four

1913
The Silk Weavers' Strike

Between 29 January and 14 August 1913 there were thirty major disputes between employers and employees in Dublin. Most involved members of James Larkin's ITGWU. There were major strikes by workers at the City of Dublin Steam Packet Company, at three of Dublin's largest coal merchants, at the ironfounders J. and C. McGloughlin and Jacob's biscuit factory. These strikes are evidence of the increasing power and influence of Larkin and the trade union movement in Dublin. Previously, employers had been able to break strikes by replacing striking workers with 'scabs' from the vast numbers of unemployed men in the city. By 1913 Larkin had succeeded in persuading 'thousands of skilled workers to subscribe to the principal that an injury to one was an injury to all', thus tipping the balance in favour of employees. The 'sympathetic strike' – strikes by separate industries in support of other striking workers – was being used effectively to secure pay increases, and improved working conditions and Larkin's power and influence was at its peak.[1] The strike of Dublin silk weavers in March 1913 was, in comparative terms, small, and one of a number underway at the same time. Nevertheless, in many ways it was a typical example of the action taken by many skilled workers in Dublin at this time.

On 12 March 1913 about one hundred men employed in the Hanbury Lane factory of Messrs Richard Atkinson and Company poplin manufacturers struck. The strike did not affect the firm's other factories at College Green or Wellington Quay. Dublin newspaper reports, appearing on 13 March, stated that the strike was restricted to members of the Silk Weavers' Union. The *Evening Telegraph* and *Evening Herald* reported that the cause of the dispute was a 'technical' one and that there were hopes of a satisfactory settlement within a few days.[2] The *Dublin Evening Mail* gave a more lengthy report claiming members of the union had 'presented a series of resolutions to the firm' which the employers were unable to accept. Although no list of the resolutions was published, it was vaguely noted that they were 'in respect of increased allowances in certain contingencies'. The reporter interviewed a 'gentleman' who stated that the question at issue was, in fact, a complicated one.[3] After these reports appeared in the evening newspapers, Mallin, as secretary of the Silk

Weavers' Union, contacted a number of newspapers in relation to the strike. On 14 March, a letter from Mallin was
published in the *Evening Telegraph* under the heading 'A City
Strike'. Mallin pointed out that there had been no demand
from the workers for an increase in wages. He also stated
that they were willing to arbitrate on the disputed matters
and suggested the Lord Mayor as a possible arbitrator, before
finishing, 'we feel confident the decision will be favourable
to the men.' The letter was signed 'Secretary' and addressed
from the 'Dublin Silk Trade Hall'.[4] On this day the *Irish Independent* and *Dublin Evening Telegraph* also announced that the
secretary of the Silk Weavers' Union had contacted them to
explain that the men were willing to submit the dispute to
arbitration. Despite these early reports, however, the dispute
never came close to a settlement in the first few days and
was to continue for a number of months. While a full list
of demands was never published, it became clear later that
a key issue was the amount of time weavers spent at looms
while waiting for material. They could not earn during these
periods and while they were not looking for an increase in
wages as such, the strike was at least partly concerned with
the amount a worker could earn in a week. It also became
clear that there were issues of principle involved and this
certainly contributed to the length of the strike.

There was much antagonism at this time between the
trade union movement and elements of the Dublin press

and this can be seen in the sometimes cloudy reporting on the strike. This antagonism is unsurprising, as the *Independent* and *Evening Herald* were owned by William Martin Murphy, head of the Dublin United Tramways group that would lock its employees out of work later in the year sparking the famous 'Dublin lockout'. The day after the strike broke out, 13 March, a deputation from the Silk Weavers' Trade Union, headed by Mallin, attended an executive meeting of the Dublin Trades Council, a council made up of representatives from Dublin's trade unions. At the meeting Mallin pointed out inaccuracies in the newspaper reports on the strike from Messrs Atkinson and Co.: the Dublin evening newspapers had reported that an early settlement was likely but this, according to Mallin, was not the case. The manager, Mallin claimed, 'refused to discuss the matter' despite the fact that the men had made three separate efforts to resolve the issue. They had 'requested a living wage'. He also pointed out that 120 men had gone on strike and eleven had remained at work in the factory and that the weavers wanted to 'place their case before the Council in order that there may be no misconception'.[5] At the next meeting, on 20 March, Mallin claimed the employers had taken 'an uncompromising attitude' in relation to the strike. He requested that the council write to Messrs Atkinson and Co. and ask that they be allowed to intervene and that he be written to at his home address of 65 Meath Street.[6]

The weavers were not the only striking workers to feel aggrieved at the way their strike was being reported: at the meeting of the Dublin Trades Council on 25 March, James Larkin gave what was described as a 'tirade' by the *Evening Telegraph*, condemning the descriptions of a strike by the Dublin steam packet workers. Larkin proposed a lengthy resolution calling on the council to regard any statements published in the *Evening Herald* as lies and as part of the 'dishonest campaign of the Dublin press'. He asked that 'until such time that a full and accurate report appears in [the *Evening Telegraph*] that no representative of said paper be allowed audience at this Trades Council.' Larkin essentially wished to ban reporters from Trades Council meetings and Mallin seconded his resolution, pointing out that the papers had inaccurately reported that the 'strike in his trade was only on a technical point, and that matter would be settled in a few days'. He was also keen to emphasise that the men were not 'cadging for their bread' as the papers may have implied. The Chairman of the Trades Council, Thomas McPartlin, was the only member to show opposition to the resolution and after a short discussion it was passed unanimously.[7] At a meeting of the Dublin Trades Council executive on 4 April, at which a deputation of silk weavers attended regarding the strike, Mallin 'referred to a report in the papers which is misleading'.[7] This comment was in relation to an article that appeared in the *Evening Telegraph* on 3 April. The article, under the heading 'Poplin

Worker's Strike, Prospects of a Settlement', claimed there were hopes that 'in the course of a few days the negotiations which have been proceeding between the employers and the workers will have a satisfactory conclusion'. The article added that there were hopes for a restoration of friendly relations between the two parties.[9] Mallin told the meeting that the dispute was not near a settlement, as Messrs Atkinson and Co. would not discuss the matter with them.

On Saturday, 5 April 1913, a notice was published in the *Irish Times* by Messrs Atkinson and Co. stating that the firm would accept applications for reinstatement from the men on strike. Applications were to be accepted until the following Tuesday, 8 May. The notice confirmed that 'all suitable weavers will be taken back at the full Trade Union rate of wages, as heretofore paid' and 'Boy apprentices over 18 years of age will be taken on as men.'[9] At this point the silk weavers had not publicly announced the reasons for their strike but the offer of full trade union wages was clearly not incentive enough as none of the men on strike were willing to accept the offer from Atkinson's. Mallin was particularly incensed by the offer to 'boy' apprentices over the age of eighteen. To Mallin this was a bribe from the company aimed at encouraging the younger weavers to agree to a settlement that did not represent the aims of the trade union. Mallin's attitude to this offer is indicative of his own strong principles and his belief in the strength of trade unionism. At a Trades Council meeting on 7 April, Mallin referred to the offer from Atkinson's, proclaiming that the silk weavers' society was 'one of the oldest in Dublin, and Messrs. Atkinson have held out a disreputable bribe to their young men.'[10] He went on to assert that the firm 'didn't want to face the matter' and 'had offered a bribe to the young men to break the union but they flouted his bribe. They threw the thing into his teeth and said they wouldn't have anything to do with it.'[11] The day before the close of applications for reinstatement, Mallin wrote an impassioned letter to the *Irish Worker* in which he referred to this 'bribe'. The letter was published under the heading 'The Bribe that Failed' and appeared on Saturday, 12 April. Mallin wrote that the offer to the boy apprentices meant an increase of between twenty-five and fifty percent in wages and the idea behind it was to 'Sell your trade union for an increase in wages'. Mallin continued, with evident pride:

> ... the reply of the apprentices is just as I was sure it would be: Keep your bribe; we want none of it. The journeyman weavers are out for the sake of our future ... Do you think we are going to sell our souls for the sake of your thirty pieces of silver? That is the spirit of our apprentices.[12]

The letter went on to describe the 'shock' of the firm as they watched fifty apprentices 'swing into Hanbury Lane with head erect defiance in their eyes ... until they met the employer who could see for himself the answer to the offer of the bribe to sell their Trade Union.' Mallin jokingly referred to the fearful reaction of the policeman on duty at the factory:'I saw him run to the door of the factory, as if to defend it: but, perhaps, it was to use its support to keep him from falling down.' He then noted that none of the men had applied for reinstatement and seven had been arrested for intimidation, or, as Mallin described it, warning the 'scabs' to 'take care or he may get entangled in the catgut of his father's fiddle strings.'[13]

By mid-April, Mallin and the men from Messrs Atkinson and Co. had been on strike for four weeks. They were, however, confident of success and unwilling to renege on their (still unpublished) demands. Mallin's letter to the *Irish Worker*, published 12 April, finished on a defiant note: 'The fight is going well. The public must not be misled on the matter. Our places cannot be filled. We are all out yet, and we will remain out until all our just demands are conceded.'[14] This defiance was also evident in Mallin's reports to the Dublin Trades Council, particularly that of 7 April, as reproduced in the *Irish Worker*. According to Mallin, Atkinson's had said they would discuss the issues if the men withdrew their list of resolutions. The men were unwilling to do this as all their complaints were contained in the resolutions and they were not willing to 'sidetrack the question at issue'. He claimed they 'would beg from door to door before they would surrender'.[15] Atkinson's were, at this point, equally defiant and neither side seemed willing to concede to the other. The dispute continued throughout the month of April and divisions between employer and employee grew.

In April, Mallin organised a number of meetings to gain support for the strike. Meetings that were to take place at Grey Square and Foster Place and be addressed by well-known Dublin trade unionists were advertised in the *Irish Worker*. Grey Square, in the Liberties of Dublin, was one area in which the Dublin silk weaving trade had been traditionally based. These meetings took place on 13 and 27 April. One of the more prominent speakers at the meeting was William Patrick Partridge, a hard-working trade unionist who was a close friend of Mallin's. In his biography of Partridge, Hugh Geraghty has noted that a threat was made to bring in army reserves to break up the dispute.[16] If such a threat was made, it was never carried out. Mallin's eldest son recalls attending one of these meetings. He recounts that during his speech, James Larkin stopped suddenly and held up the poplin tie he was wearing. In a typical theatrical gesture, he apologised for wearing a product made by Atkinson's and offered to tear off the offending item. Mallin took hold of the tie and examined it, before remarking: 'Do not mind wearing it, Elliot's made it.'[17]

At this time another divisive issue arose. As none of the employees had applied for reinstatement by 8 April, Messrs Atkinson and Co. began to employ new workers to replace them. As early as 9 April the Dublin evening newspapers reported that the firm had begun taking on new men and boys to replace those on strike. The firm intended to fill the places gradually as the new employees would have to be fully trained in the technical aspects of the work and as a result it would be impossible to replace all the workers immediately.[18] The *Irish Times* also reported that Messrs Atkinson and Co. had made arrangements to fill the vacant positions and stated 'the strikers have placed themselves outside the consideration of the firm.'[19] Furthermore, the firm made it clear they were unwilling to give way to the workers and emphasised their 'determination to prevent … any interference with the men they have engaged.' It was not the busy season in the trade and, as such, the firm were able to meet all the orders they had received. The firm also stated their disappointment at the stance of the strikers, as they had trained the majority of the men into the business.[20] The dispute was growing more acute at this point and the chances of a settlement were remote. The policy of bringing in new men would create a major point of contention during the attempts to influence a settlement that followed later. As the new employees began working at the factory those on strike were keen to disrupt them and encourage them not to work for the firm. These attempts often took on a violent nature. Just days after Atkinson's began rehiring, a number of the men on strike were arrested for attempting to intimidate some of the new men.[21] On the evening of 10 April a window of one of the employees' homes in Weaver's Square was smashed; no arrests were made.[22]

Despite the levels of tension at the beginning of the month, by the end of April the employers and employees of Messrs Atkinson and Co. began negotiations on a settlement. On Monday, 21 April a meeting was held in the Mansion House, Dublin, with the Lord Mayor of Dublin, Lorcan Sherlock, presiding and two representatives from each side present. Michael Mallin was almost certainly present as a representative of the silk weavers. The negotiations produced an agreement on all of the issues in question until the end of the meeting when a point of disagreement was raised. The workers were unhappy that the men who did not go on strike were not to be 'penalised'. According to the *Evening Telegraph*, the workers 'put forward the claim that there should be "discipline" among the members of the Union.'[23] Clearly, at least some of the men who had not gone on strike had been in the union. The next day the *Evening Telegraph* reported that negotiations had broken off and the firm were continuing on their business, although at a reduced rate due to 'a shortage of hands, but this is gradually being remedied'.[24] During further negotiations that Thursday the employees had agreed not to pursue punishment against their colleagues who had stayed at work, but this did not produce a final settlement. Messrs Atkinson and Co. had hired twelve workers during the strike and wanted to retain all twelve. Those who had gone on strike, however, were unwilling to work alongside 'scabs' who had crossed the picket. Mallin told the Trades Council he 'objected to the retention of these 12 men who must go before they (the silkweavers) resume work. That is the point they are fighting on.' The Trades Council supported the Silk Weavers' Union in this and Mr O'Brien of the Labourers Union proposed the motion:

> That this Trades Council condemns the attitude taken up by Messrs Atkinson and Co. in their attempt to force into the Weaver's Union some ten or twelve scabs, and call upon the trades societies to further assist the Dublin silk weavers financially so that they may be able to beat the firm in their attempt against trade unionism.[25]

The motion was seconded and then passed. A further point of grievance for the employees was the fact that, as was claimed, the firm intended the returning men to train the new employees in the trade. According to Mallin, 'It would be three years before those scabs could be trusted to do anything for themselves, and only half of them would be likely to become weavers.'[26] Despite being as near to a settlement as they had been throughout the strike, the union members remained defiant on this issue and as a result the strike was prolonged for a number of weeks.

By the beginning of June the strike was still underway

and was into its twelfth week. Mallin had a letter published in the *Irish Worker* on 31 May in which he wrote, 'What a beautiful farce this fight has degenerated into.' In a somewhat angry tone Mallin described how two of the men, Michael and Tom Byrne, had 'proved themselves traitors' after eleven weeks. Michael Byrne was, apparently, about eighty-six years old and Mallin scornfully commented: 'what a beautiful heading for his tombstone – Scab R.I.P.'. The letter finished positively: 'One hundred good and true men are still in the fight, and mean to fight it out. The principle of Trades Unionism depends on it.'[27] This letter again emphasises Mallin's commitment to the principles of trade unionism, but also highlights his firmness and a willingness to dismiss those not equally committed to the cause.

At this time the Lord Mayor of Dublin, Lorcan Sherlock, approached both sides in an attempt to reopen negotiations. At a meeting of the Dublin Corporation on 2 June, William Partridge brought the matter of the strike forward for discussion. Partridge stated that during the previous negotiations the employers had agreed that the cause for the strike was justified. Furthermore, he added that 'when the question arose as to removing those who had replaced the men who went out on strike, the employers stated that there would be no difficulty getting over the matter.' He added that the Lord Mayor had also confirmed this. Partridge felt the Lord Mayor had been 'lacking in his duty' as he had not enforced these terms on Atkinson's. In response, the Lord Mayor argued that Partridge's statement had been 'partly right and partly wrong'. He claimed that both sides had approached him to call a conference. The Lord Mayor then went on to say he had been told, in private, that the firm were willing to remove the new employees before adding that he did not expect 'self-respecting men who had gone out on strike on a question of principle to work side by side with the men who took their place.'[28]

Michael Mallin referred to the Lord Mayor's comments at the next meeting of the Dublin Trades Council. Mallin argued that, in his reply to Partridge, it was the Lord Mayor who was, in fact, 'part right and part wrong'. Mallin believed the Lord Mayor had not been as fair as he had hoped and claimed Sherlock was 'driving a bargain with the employer behind their backs.' The Lord Mayor had written a letter to the Trades Council asking that they send a delegation for an informal conference on the strike. It was then agreed that a committee including Thomas McPartlin and James Larkin should attend.[29] Messrs Atkinson and Co. also responded to the Lord Mayor's comments at the Corporation meeting. The firm asked for a letter to be published in a number of Dublin evening newspapers. In this letter, Atkinson's firstly noted that the firm had not approached the Lord Mayor (Sherlock later apologised for his comments and stated that it was he who had approached both parties in a letter to the

Irish Times on 9 June). Atkinson's claimed they were willing to meet the men, but this could not be considered arbitration due to the treatment suffered by the men who had not gone on strike and those who had been employed during the strike. In relation to the Lord Mayor's claims that he had been promised there would be no difficulty removing the new men, while attempting not to 'impugn the Lord Mayor's good faith', Atkinson's maintained 'no such proposal was ever contemplated by us, nor was any such statement made to him.'[30] It is unclear whether a member of the firm had told the Lord Mayor this and it was simply later denied, but Mallin, Partridge and the men on strike had all been led to believe the firm were willing to remove and compensate the new employees. Messrs Atkinson and Co., however, felt differently.

Despite the controversy surrounding the Lord Mayor's comments and the apparent unwillingness of either side to back down on the issue of the new employees, negotiations continued. After a conference on 12 June, exactly four months after the men had left work, it was reported that the strike had been settled and they would return to work on the following Monday. It was decided not to make the results of the settlement public. John Grogan announced to the Dublin Trades Council that the dispute between Messrs Atkinson and Co. and the silk weavers had been 'brought to a satisfactory conclusion'. Mallin thanked the other trade unions for their support during the strike.[31] Although the exact terms of the settlement were not disclosed, it must be seen as a success for the Silk Weavers' Union. Grogan declared the workers had 'won considerable concessions'. It appears the final grievance – the position of the new employees – also went in favour of the workers. Mallin told a Trades Council meeting of 16 June, as reported in the *Irish Worker*:

> a statement that appeared in the 'Daily Express', to the effect that the men taken on during the strike would be kept on … was an absolute fabrication. He communicated with Mr. Swirles (Manager, Atkinson's) and he denied being responsible for the statement.[32]

This would suggest that the firm had conceded on this point. Michael Mallin was the principal figure behind the strike and the fact that the men were able to stay out of work for thirteen weeks was in no small way due to his organisational work and the support of the Dublin Trades Council and the trade unions of Dublin. Mallin made sure the council were aware of their dispute and repeatedly appealed for financial assistance, pointing out how crucial it was to their success.[33] The Trades Council supported the men on strike generously. A fund was set up levying one penny per member towards the silk weavers' strike and a committee established to deal with the money to include James Larkin.[34]

The case of the workers also reached a wide audience and

Mallin must take some credit for this. During the Labour Day meeting in the Phoenix Park, Walter Hall, of the National Union of Railwaymen, referred to the silk weaver's strike. He appealed for support and said 'it should always be present in their minds the struggle these people were engaged in.'[35] In reference to this, Mr O'Brien pointed out to the Trades Council that 'in the Park on Labour Day every Trade Unionist there held up his hand and declared their determination that they would not allow the weavers to go down.'[36] Thomas McPartlin, President of the Dublin Trades Council, also brought the strike to the attention of the delegates at the 1913 Irish Trades Union Congress, held in Cork in May. McPartlin described the strike as 'one of principle' and appealed to the delegates for support.

The silk weavers' strike can be seen as one of a number of industrial disputes in Dublin during the first half of 1913 essentially serving as a backdrop to events that culminated in the most famous Irish labour dispute, the Dublin lockout. In August 1913 a group of employers, headed by William Martin Murphy, tried to force its employees to sign a declaration that they would withdraw from the ITGWU. In response, the ITGWU called other workers out on strike and soon some twenty thousand workers in the city were either on strike or locked out of work.

As he was not directly affected by the lockout, the weaver's strike is also significant in terms of Mallin's development.

Firstly, it is likely that it was the only large-scale trade dispute in which he was directly involved and it contributed greatly to his reputation as a trade union organiser. Secondly, it offers a revealing glimpse of one important character trait. Despite the ultimate success of the strike, the long weeks out of earning must have put a considerable strain on Mallin's young family. Mallin's commitment to the strike, particularly as it descended into one increasingly based on 'principle' is evidence of a total dedication to the cause. This is a dedication that Mallin expected not only of himself, but of those around him.

Chapter 5

1913 – 1914
Changing Fortunes; Joining the ITGWU; Character

According to eldest his son, Michael Mallin left Atkinson's not long after the silk weavers' strike. It is not clear if he lost his job there or resigned. Around this time the family also sold their shop in Meath Street.[1] In R.M. Fox's *The History of the Irish Citizen Army*, it is claimed that the shop was closed 'owing to the poverty of his working-class customers'. The Dublin lockout was underway and thousands of Dublin's workers were either locked out of work or on strike; these men and their families were unable to afford luxury items such as newspapers and tobacco.[2] Mallin also seems to have lost another class of customer around the same time. In August 1913 newsboys in the employment of William Martin Murphy's newspaper company went on strike. The strike resulted in a number of violent clashes with police as the newsboys attacked *Evening Herald* delivery vans with large paving stones. This strike was, according to James O'Shea, 'the first time Mike Mallon [sic] got up against the police'. Mallin's shop had a number of regular police customers. On one occasion a sergeant ('a brute would be a respectable term to use in this case') was openly discussing what they would do to end the newsboys' strike. Hearing this, states O'Shea, 'Mike attacked him, the Police and the Government and there was a great showdown in his shop. The consequence was that Mike's name was discussed in Newmarket Police station and police customers thereafter were few and far between.'[3] This would suggest that Mallin left Meath Street some time shortly after August 1913.

According to Séamus Mallin, his father briefly considered moving to Australia after they sold the shop. James O'Shea recalls that Mallin actually discussed the possibility of moving to 'Argentina or some South American state. He said he would never be able to stick Ireland as she was at that time.'[4] The choice to stay, perhaps, stemmed from his political beliefs and his desire to improve conditions in Ireland. In his final letter to his wife on the eve of his execution, Mallin made a gloomy reference to this decision: 'if only I had taken your advice and left the Country we might have been so happy but Ireland always came first.'[5]

Having sold the shop, Mallin made the unusual decision

to move to Finglas, at that time a small village surrounded by open countryside, and establish a chicken farm. The money from the sale of the shop was invested in a house about a mile beyond the village, in chicken coops and a collection of Rhode Island Reds and other breeds of chicken. Mallin, however, had no luck in this venture. Shortly after the move, he contracted Bright's disease, a kidney disease that proved near fatal. Any money left from the sale of the shop went on doctor's fees and medical bills and the family were forced to return to the city in spring 1914, where Mallin began weaving again (probably from a loom at home). Another shop was opened in Upper Kevin Street. They would not stay long there either, however, opening yet another shop in Francis Street later that year.[6]

In one of his articles about his father, published by *Inniu* in 1966, Séamus Mallin wrote of his father: 'There were always plans forming in the head of my father. There was no limit on him. But they rarely worked when put into practice.' He also commented on how the financial shortcomings of his father's schemes sometimes made life difficult for the family. Several closed shops and a failed chicken farm were not the only business ventures Mallin attempted. His son has described how he opened a cinema on the corner of Mary Street and Jervis Street. He remembers watching films featuring American policeman running about, but also the difficulty his father had with the modern, electric lighting and that it was forced to close down, losing the family a sub-stantial amount of money.[7] Although there is no surviving evidence to link Mallin directly to a picture house in Dublin, that Séamus Mallin remembers visiting the cinema should allow for an assumption that it did exist. In December 1909 a cinema was opened on Mary Street, four shop fronts (number 45) from the corner of Jervis Street: James Joyce, author of *Ulysses*, had secured foreign investment and the Volta Electric Picturehouse was opened with Joyce as manager. Joyce's stint in the world of cinema was, however, a short-lived one and after seven months, having grown bored and restless with the project, he resigned. The Volta was in a number of dif-ferent hands before 1916. Mallin was almost certainly never involved in the running of the Volta, however. A more likely candidate is the Irish Cinema, opened around 1912 in 113 Capel Street, a short distance from Mary Street and Jervis Street and next to the Trades Hall (Mallin had earlier owned a shop at number 111). The Irish Cinema, owned and man-aged in 1912 by R.H. Graham, featured in the 'Pictures in Ireland' column, written by 'Paddy' in the British industry newspaper *Bioscope*.[8] An advertisement for the cinema regu-larly appeared in the *Irish Worker* newspaper, urging workers to visit 'the Only Picture House in Dublin owned by an Irishman'. Graham (who was fined on a number of occasions for various misdemeanours) was still running the cinema in July 1915. That month Graham was taken to court over the non-payment of £60 rent. In his defence Graham claimed that business had been directly affected by the outbreak of the Great War the year before. Prior to the war, takings averaged £11 a week but had dropped to £6 and Graham was now losing £1 a week on the cinema. He was hoping to the sell the premises but this was impossible until the winter as 'Even if the war were never on, one could never sell a picture house in the summer.'[9] The fate of the Irish Cinema after this is unclear. It is possible that Mallin bought the cinema from Graham in 1915 (unwisely, given Graham's own statements in court) and ran it himself from then. This would mean a very brief undertaking as Mallin would certainly have closed the cinema prior to the build-up to the Rising. Another possibility is that Mallin was a partner of Graham's. With the fall in takings and arrears of rent due, the cinema may have been closed in 1915, meaning Mallin lost whatever investment he had made. A further prospect, and perhaps a more feasible one, is that Mallin operated one of the many unlicensed or unregistered cinema houses that grew up around Dublin in the nineteen tens. These houses usually went unrecorded, unless the owner was prosecuted. Mallin's cinema may have sprung up, on the site named by Séamus Mallin, and been closed down without any official record ever existing.

ITGWU

The Irish Transport and General Workers' Union was established in December 1908 by James Larkin and drew its membership from a wide range of trades and industries. In October 1914 James Connolly became acting general secretary of the union, replacing Larkin who had decided to leave for America. Between October 1914 and May 1915 Michael Mallin became increasingly involved in the ITGWU. Although exact dates are difficult to establish for this period of Mallin's life, it is possible to recreate an account of Mallin's growing involvement with the ITGWU.

The Inchicore branch of the ITGWU was under the leadership of a close friend of Mallin's, William Partridge. The union ran a band, the Emmet Fife and Drum Band, from its premises – the Emmet Hall, Emmet Road, Inchicore. Around May 1914 Mallin took over as conductor of this band. He may also have become a member of the union around this time. In his Inchicore notes for the *Irish Worker*, Partridge announced that Mallin had taken over and that 'rapid progress' was expected. He requested new members to join immediately as preparations were under way for the Labour Day demonstrations, due to take place on 31 May.[10] Under Mallin, the Emmet Fife and Drum Band practised every Tuesday and Friday evening. This was coupled with the drilling taking place for the Inchicore branch of the Irish Citizen Army, in which Mallin was likely involved. Partridge used his column in the *Irish Worker* to report on the progress of the band. On 2 May, Partridge wrote, 'Wonderful progress is being made under Mr. Mallin's able tuition and it is confidently expected that the band will take its place in the Labour demonstration.'[11] A week later Partridge was able to report that the band's appearance at the demonstrations was 'definitely assured.'[12] The Labour Day demonstration of 1914 took place on 31 May with roughly four thousand members of Dublin trade unions involved. A procession marched from Sackville (now O'Connell) Street to the Phoenix Park in Dublin. The trade unions from the Inchicore area marched to Parnell Square and from there joined the march to the Phoenix Park.[13]

Mallin's first association with the ITGWU coincides with the end of his service as secretary of the Dublin Silk Weavers' Trade Union. Soon after he began conducting the Emmet Fife and Drum Band, at a meeting in July 1914, Mallin was removed from the position. Unhappy with the decision, Mallin refused to return the union's books. On 7 August he was summoned to the Southern Police Court by union chairman Charles Farrell. The union claimed that, dissatisfied with his conduct, they had decided to dispense with his services and passed a resolution to that effect, also demanding the return of their books. According to the union, 'Mr. Mallin had not been conducting the affairs of the society as they ought to have been conducted: that they were unable to get the books audited, and that owing to his conduct the Society's affairs were in a state of chaos.' Mallin's defence argued that he was dismissed at a meeting where the required number of delegates was not present, invalidating the vote. It was argued that Mallin was ousted by an unhappy minority. Nevertheless, newspaper reports of the court sitting confirmed that the case was 'dismissed without prejudice' and that the society could proceed for 'legal detention of the books'.[14] Either explanation for Mallin's dismissal (and there may be an element of truth in both), may be the result of his growing radicalism. Perhaps his work as secretary suffered as he became more involved in militarism and perhaps a number of his union colleagues noticed this shift and became worried or unhappy; not long afterwards, Mallin became the first Chief-of-Staff of the Irish Citizen Army.

In late 1914 Mallin was approached by James Connolly and offered the job of manager of the Emmet Hall in Inchicore, which had been vacated by William Partridge.[15] There was an apartment and a shop attached to the hall, and the Mallin family moved in there and, continuing a trend, established a newsagent's. Mallin had already been involved in the Emmet Fife and Drum Band there. The site, adjacent to Richmond barracks, also offered a convenient location from which to secure firearms from soldiers, something Mallin appears to have had a talent for. This was, perhaps, taken into account when Connolly offered Mallin the job.

James O'Shea, a close associate of Mallin, has described how at the time at which Mallin became active in Inchicore the ITGWU 'was at its lowest ebb' as James Larkin was preparing to go to America and they were hearing about James Connolly 'but knew little of him'. This, however, 'did not shake Mike Mallin'. During a discussion with O'Shea in Emmet Hall, Mallin outlined his desire to rebuild the union and, in O'Shea's words, 'He had plans *go loer* [sic]'. Despite the unfavourable circumstances (even O'Shea has admitted that he could not 'see eye to eye' with Mallin's plans due to the weak state of the union at the time) Mallin's enthusiasm and commitment is obvious.[16]

In May 1915 James Connolly visited ITGWU branches in Wexford, Waterford, Cork and Belfast. In his report to the committee on his trip Connolly suggested that 'a man be appointed to pay occasional visits to these places to keep them stirred up.' He recommended that William Partridge, head of the Inchicore branch, be appointed as countrywide organiser to hold meetings and 'work them up'.[17] The appointment of Partridge as an organiser for branches around the country was confirmed at the next committee meeting on 19 May. At that meeting Connolly announced that it was necessary to replace Partridge as head of the Inchicore branch and that he had given the position to 'Mr. Mallon [sic] of the Silk Weavers Union'. The Inchicore branch of the ITGWU was run from Emmet Hall. Connolly explained that Mallin had been given the position as 'he was living on the premises and would be there at all times to look after the branch.' This was moved by P. Forde, seconded by James Kelly and passed unanimously.[18] This marks an upgrade from Mallin's previous role of manager of the building to organiser for the whole branch. Unfortunately, no records of the Inchicore ITGWU branch have survived and it is therefore impossible to assess how active Mallin was in this role and how the branch was run after the departure of Partridge.

There is, however, evidence of at least one function Mallin performed in this role. At the same meeting at which Mallin was appointed, James Connolly recommended that the union hold a conference of delegates to meet at least four times a year. The first of these was to take place on Whit Sunday 1915.[19] A representative of each branch of the ITGWU attended this conference, which took place in Liberty Hall on 24 May 1915. Michael Mallin attended as the representative for Inchicore. At the meeting all delegates were asked to speak and to give an account of the condition of their branch. The surviving minutes of the meeting detail speeches made by a number of delegates, but none from Mallin. It is unclear whether Mallin spoke at the meeting at all.[20] It is possible that as the conference took place five days after Mallin had been appointed, he felt unable to give an accurate summary of the condition of the branch.

Character

Mallin was a strongly principled man who could be strict and impatient with those who did not match his commitment and discipline. He was also easily offended when it came to his political or religious beliefs. His son, Séamus, has emphasised this aspect of his father's character. On one occasion Mallin brought Séamus to a variety performance. One of the actors made a joke about 'Skin the Goat' (James Fitzharris). 'Skin the Goat' was a member of the Invincibles, an extreme nationalist society. In November 1881 members of the society killed the Irish Chief Secretary and Under-Secretary in the Phoenix Park. 'Skin the Goat' drove the carriage that brought the killers to the park on the night and spent fifteen years in prison, refusing to name any of his colleagues. On hearing the joke, Mallin apparently stood up and declared, 'I will not stay here listening to a clown abuse Skin the Goat to get a laugh from people', and left, dragging his young son behind. On another occasion, Mallin was furious to learn that his father had brought Séamus home one night on a tram; the tram company was owned by William Martin Murphy, an enemy of Dublin trade unionists. Mallin also harboured a particular dislike for the Dublin Metropolitan Police and was again furious when one of his sons fell into a small pond in the Phoenix Park and was dragged out by a man who turned out to be a policeman.

He was, however, also a kind and gentle father. One of his

concerts was twice interrupted by a young Séamus Mallin, who let out a great scream each time the music started. Séamus remembers that his father 'put a stop to the noise I was making and tried to find out what was the cause. I was not able to say a word, but I recall my father was very patient and very kind with me.' Later, during an Irish Citizen Army training session in Croydon Park, a member fired a gun without permission and the bullet entered Séamus Mallin's foot (the men remarked that he was 'the first casualty of the war'). Séamus immediately knew that his father would be livid with whoever had fired without permission, but Mallin said nothing at the time, more concerned with his injured son. He later gave him half a crown 'for being brave', while unsurprisingly venting his anger at the men some time later.[21]

Those who knew Michael Mallin described him as a rather short, dapper man with a kind, sensitive manner and a gentle voice. William Partridge, in a letter to his wife from Lewes prison in December 1916 after he had been asked to be godfather to Mallin's daughter Maura, wrote: 'It is an honour indeed to stand sponsor for the offspring of one of the finest – most kindly hearted – and clean minded men it has ever been my good fortune to meet.'[22] Mallin was deeply religious, sensitive, a teetotaller who disliked swearing, a skilled silk weaver, a music teacher and an avid reader of the history of South America, ancient Europe and the novels of Joseph Conrad. He may not have immediately struck one as a soldier. Nora Connolly O'Brien, daughter of James Connolly, recalls that when she heard Mallin was to become Chief-of-Staff of the Irish Citizen Army she remarked, 'He is such a gentle person, it's hard to think of him as a great soldier.'[23] But when he was appointed to the role in October 1914, he had spent over a quarter of his life as a soldier in the British army and had made a rapid rise through the ranks of the Irish Citizen Army to become second-in-command.

Chapter 6

1914 – 1916
Irish Citizen Army

The Irish Citizen Army (ICA) was founded by the Irish Transport and General Workers' Union (ITGWU) to protect demonstrating workers from the Dublin Metropolitan Police (DMP) during the Dublin lockout. Strikes and pickets that were formed during the lockout were often subject to violent interventions from the DMP, including baton charges. After a particularly brutal confrontation in Sackville (O'Connell) Street a meeting was called to denounce the actions of the police. At this meeting, the formation of a citizen army was suggested by Captain J.R. White. White was an experienced military man who had won a Distinguished Service Order, one of the highest British army honours for gallantry, and was full of energy, passion and enthusiasm.

The first function of the newly established force was the protection of Dublin workers from police brutality during strikes or at meetings. Originally led by James Larkin, found-ing members included the playwright Sean O'Casey and Countess Markievicz. The pacifist Francis Sheehy-Skeffing-ton was another founding member, but he left the organisa-tion in early 1914 when it began to shift from its original role as a protection force to a more military route.

The first phase of the ICA's existence revolved around drilling, led by Captain White in Croydon Park, and protec-tion duties at union parades and marches. Soon, however, White left the organisation, frustrated at the poor attendance of members at drilling.

The foundation of the ICA, about a month before the Irish Volunteers were set up was characteristic of the increased militarism of a period when organisations were founded to fight for or protect political interests north and south of the country. At its peak the ICA numbered around 350, the majority of its members drawn from Dublin trade unions.[1] According to Mallin's brother, Thomas, Michael was not a member of the Citizen Army at this point. He recalls a conversation with James Larkin about the acquisition of guns during the early days of the force and is certain that his brother was not a member when this conversation took place.[2] The exact date that Mallin joined the ICA remains unclear.

In late 1914 the ICA and trade unionism in Dublin were in a poor position. The ITGWU was heavily in debt and many of its members were suffering dire poverty. By October 1914, the ICA was similarly disorganised, demoralised and ineffectual. On 24 October James Larkin announced that he was leaving for America to raise funds for the ITGWU. James Connolly was to take charge of the workers' army. This marked a new phase in the history of the ICA. It is from this point that the small army began to take the shape of the body that would participate in insurrection in less than two years' time. Connolly immediately set about shaping the 'fermenting yeast' of the ICA into a vanguard for revolution.[3] Soon after Connolly took control, Michael Mallin was appointed as his new Chief-of-Staff. Under Connolly, there was no systematic attempt to grow the numbers of the army. The key qualities of the organisation, for Connolly, were a definite commitment to revolution and a willingness to take to the field at short notice. While Connolly was the ideological and philosophical head of the movement, 'he left the business of organisation and training to Michael Mallin.'[4]

Mallin's first recorded involvement with the ICA came in 1914. James O'Shea relates how he had a long discussion with Mallin in the Emmet Hall, Inchicore, during which Mallin asked him to join a branch of the ICA he was planning to set up. O'Shea claims the conversation came about at a time when 'everything was at its lowest ebb. Jim Larkin was about to go to America and the Union only existed in Liberty Hall. We were then getting to hear a lot of Jim Connolly, but knew little of him.'[5] This would suggest that this was in the latter half of 1914, after the collapse of the lockout and before Larkin's departure in October. A branch of the Irish Citizen Army was founded at the Emmet Hall and officially launched on 1 February 1914 by Captain Jack White and William Partridge.[6] It is unclear whether this is the same branch Mallin discussed with O'Shea. Regardless, Mallin's group seems to have been a small one, as O'Shea remembers:

> ... we started with about 12 or 14; we drilled twice a week and often walked on a Saturday from Inchicore to Croydon Park to carry out drill etc. It was tough for some time, but after a little time we got some rifles, Italian thumb lock; they were heavy and awkward but great for drilling and we thought them magnificent though there was no ammunition for them.[7]

O'Shea also recalls Mallin's enthusiasm, even as the numbers of recruits dropped: 'The smaller we became the more active Mike Mallin became. He used to give us lectures and we were becoming real soldiers. He lectured us on outpost duty and brought us out to the park at night'.[8] There is no other extant evidence for Mallin's ICA activity aside from the small branch recalled by O'Shea. If this was Mallin's sole role within the organisation prior to October 1914, then his appointment as Chief-of-Staff represents a somewhat meteoric rise through the ranks. Why then did Connolly choose Mallin as his second-in-command? The most obvious answer is Mallin's military experience, having served for thirteen years in the British army. When Connolly took control of the ICA his aim was to turn it into a military force capable of participating in an armed revolution. Therefore, military experience was essential to prepare the organisation for this. Mallin seemed to share Connolly's outlook and 'regarded the Citizen Army as a practical military force for use in the near future'.[9] Connolly's daughter, Ina, has recalled her father's response to a woman distraught that her son had joined the British army:

> Many a good man was in the British army; there is nothing wrong in being well-trained and it is in the British army the soldier gets a good training. It's getting out of the army in time of peace and putting your knowledge to the advantage of your country is what I call a good soldier.[10]

Connolly himself had spent time in the British army and other Citizen Army officers, such as Richard McCormick, John O'Neill and Christopher and Vincent Poole, also held military experience.

Though it is not clear when Connolly and Mallin first met, Connolly was certainly aware of Mallin before October 1914 through Mallin's involvement with socialism in Dublin and his leadership of the weavers' strike in 1913. The qualities that Mallin would later display as Chief-of-Staff must have been obvious to Connolly at this time: enthusiasm, work rate, discipline and ability to train and drill men effectively. In *Portrait of a Rebel Father*, Connolly's daughter, Nora Connolly O'Brien, imaginatively recreates the scene when her father told her that he had 'discovered a great military man ... Michael Mallin ... The way he handled his men [on manoeuvres] was splendid. His instruction to them showed he has a great grip on military matters.'[11] It is likely that ability was a deciding factor, as Mallin and Connolly do not seem to have had a close personal relationship, even after October 1914; Nora Connolly O'Brien's account hints more at respect than friendship. An often-quoted anecdote from Frank Robbins paints a revealing picture of their relationship. Robbins wrote that Mallin, who had contracted malaria in India that occasionally made him appear intoxicated, was suffering the side-effects one day and Connolly, misinterpreting the symptoms, rebuked Mallin for being under the influence of alcohol. Mallin was apparently so hurt and disappointed at Connolly's lack of trust that he decided not to mention the malaria to Connolly.[12]

After his appointment, in R.M. Fox's words, Mallin along with Connolly became 'the mainspring of the Citizen Army' (in his introduction to *The History of the Irish Citizen Army*, Fox described Mallin as 'a star on the folds of its flag').[13] Notwithstanding their strikingly different personalities, Connolly and Mallin shared a common vision for the

ICA and changes in the force soon became apparent. Frank Robbins, a committed member, has recalled that prior to Connolly's taking over, the ICA was as notable for its poor time-keeping as anything else. Robbins remembers parades starting up to an hour after the appointed time and Connolly's sarcastic commentary: 'I can always guarantee that the Irish Citizen Army will fight, but I cannot guarantee that they will be in time for such a fight when it takes place.'[14] With Mallin's appointment, Robbins notes, 'the laxity disappeared', along with some members who were less favourable to the requirements of the new regime.

Under Connolly and Mallin the training of the ICA became increasingly efficient. Drilling increased and Sundays and bank holidays were used for outdoor exercises in the mountains and in County Dublin. Connolly and Mallin lectured the men on different forms of guerrilla warfare. Mock battles and attacks on buildings took place, including a midnight mock attack on Dublin Castle in late 1915. 'We were improved out of all semblance of what we were when Jim Connolly and Mick Mallon [sic] took over,' noted James O'Shea. 'We were now thoroughly trained soldiers well drilled in the rifle and plenty of lectures in street fighting and house fighting.' O'Shea has described the type of training that took place in the Dublin mountains under Mallin:

The companies were marching in fours along a country road and at the whistle and an order 'prepare for cavalry'

both sides of the road were manned by squads of 8, four
men kneeling and four standing. The men kneeling and
standing had bayonets fixed. We reformed then and marched
along and at an order 'rally' we surrounded Mallin forming
a square of steel. It was very interesting when we were told
this method would hold cavalry and beat an attack if there
was no wavering.[15]

One member of the ICA, however, was less keen on the
training regime. Thomas O'Donoghue, in his statement to
the Bureau of Military History, has claimed, 'The result of
my participation in manoeuvres was that I had very little
respect for the ability of the officers of the Citizen Army…
the majority, as trained soldiers of the British army, lacked
initiative and the practical knowledge of strategy and tactics.'
O'Donoghue describes one manoeuvre in north County
Dublin during which Mallin was in charge of a party defending the city. O'Donoghue claims that his own attacking group
used a 'skeleton party' to hold up Mallin's forces while the rest
attacked and 'According to the rules of warfare, Commandant Mallin's party would have been captured.' When criticised afterwards by O'Donoghue, Mallin apparently claimed
he 'objected to De Wet tactics'.[16] Christiaan Rudolf de Wet
was a famous Boer leader during the Boer War – a significant
point of interest for those in Ireland interested in military
affairs at this time, though exactly which tactics Mallin was
referring to is not made clear by O'Donoghue. This is the

only real evidence of any criticism of Mallin to be found among statements made by members of the ICA. By way of explanation it may be worth noting here that O'Donoghue was a founding member of Fianna Éireann. The leaders of the scouting movement in 1909 had, apparently, distrusted Mallin as an ex-British army member and O'Donoghue's comments may be linked to that period. That O'Donoghue fancied himself as somewhat of a military tactician and displayed a personal dislike for ex-British soldiers may also be significant.[17] Despite O'Donoghue's reservations, Mallin was widely considered to be an effective and well-respected leader. An article in the *Workers' Republic* relating to a display by the ICA stated, 'To single out any one individual for praise in connection with the event would perhaps be invidious, but no one will grudge a vote of thanks being moved to our popular Chief-of-Staff.'[18] An earlier article about the procession to the grave of Theobald Wolfe Tone on 21 May 1915, in which the ICA and Irish Volunteers took part notes, 'Mr. Mallin, as Chief-of-Staff of the Citizen Army, carried out his duties in a manner that earned the praise of all.'[19]

By June 1915 the ICA were taking part in national competitions alongside the Irish Volunteers. One such event, or *feis*, took place in Tullow, County Carlow. The trip to Tullow was, perhaps, more noteworthy than the *feis* itself. The men who were to take part in the competition had spent Saturday night camped in Croydon Park before making their way to Kingsbridge station (now Heuston station) on Sunday morning. They had cleaned and polished their equipment and, as Sunday was a wet morning, had left their gear in a dry shed before attending mass. The men returned from mass to find a cow attempting to eat a ball of ammunition. When they arrived at Kingsbridge, Mallin was told the train was full. Refusing to accept this, he informed the station master that the train would not leave unless two special carriages were put on for the Citizen Army men. He then posted men to keep guard over the engine, and the driver and fireman were forced to step down. When informed by the station-master that he would bring the police, Mallin apparently advised him to bring the military too. The requested carriages were soon supplied.[20] On arrival in Tullow the first ICA team won first prize for drill – an impressive achievement, as Frank Robbins has noted that 'most of the team had known nothing of the business end of a rifle twelve or eighteen months prior to that date.' At another event in St Enda's school, Rathfarnham, at which William Pearse, Éamon de Valera and Mallin were judges, the ICA team were beaten into second place as Mallin had taken marks from them himself: 'he felt justified in doing so because of his military experience,' recalled Robbins.[21]

According to Robbins, an important morale-boosting element of ICA activity were the concerts held by members in Liberty Hall each Sunday evening. Plays from the Abbey

A young Michael Mallin
in the uniform of the
Royal Scots Fusiliers.
Mallin served in the
British army from 1889
to 1902.

Soldier's Name and Description on Attestation.

*Name Michael Mallin
Enlisted for the Royal Scots Fusrs
on the 21st October 1889
at Dublin
for 12 years in the Army and ___ years in the Reserve,
in the County of Dublin
at the age of 14 years ___ months.
Born in the Parish of St Catherines
in or near the Town of } Dublin
in the County of
Trade or Calling ___
Last permanent Residence Dublin
Height 4 Feet 5 Inches.
Complexion Fresh
Eyes Grey   Hair Brown
Marks
†Religion Roman Catholic
‡Signature of Soldier M Mallin

*The Soldier's number, name, and corps should be distinctly written on the cover of
this book. Every Soldier is to communicate to his friends the regimental number by which
he is known, and to acquaint them, that in all inquiries which they make after him,
whether addressed to the Regiment or to the War Office, they are to state such number.
† This should be described under one of the following headings, viz. :—" Church
of England," "Presbyterian." "Weslyan." "Other Protestants," or "Roman
Catholic." "Jew"
‡ Whenever a Soldier who cannot write makes his mark in acknowledgment of
having received Pay or Allowances, etc., such mark is to be witnessed.

Left: Mallin's account book or pocket ledger from his time with the Royal Scots Fusiliers. He joined up when he was fourteen years of age and four feet five inches tall.

Below: A Christmas card from Michael Mallin to Agnes Hickey from India, where he was stationed with the British army.

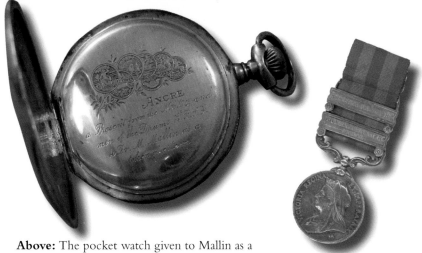

Above: The pocket watch given to Mallin as a gift on his discharge from the British army in 1902. The inscription reads: 'A present from the N.C.Os. and men of the Drums 1ˢᵗ R.S.F. to Dr[ummer] M. Mallin as a token of esteem.'

Top right: Mallin's medal from the Tirah campaign. Having received the medal, Mallin wrote to Agnes, 'I am very proud dear to have a medal but would be far prouder if it was for Ireland I earned it'.

Right: Agnes Mallin (*née* Hickey). Mallin met Agnes Hickey while on leave from the British army. They were married in 1903.

Left: Mallin in his late twenties when he left the British army and began his trade as a silk weaver.

Below: Poor Dublin children being fed by a nun. Poverty was endemic in the city at the turn of the twentieth century. Mallin would have witnessed this kind of poverty first-hand.

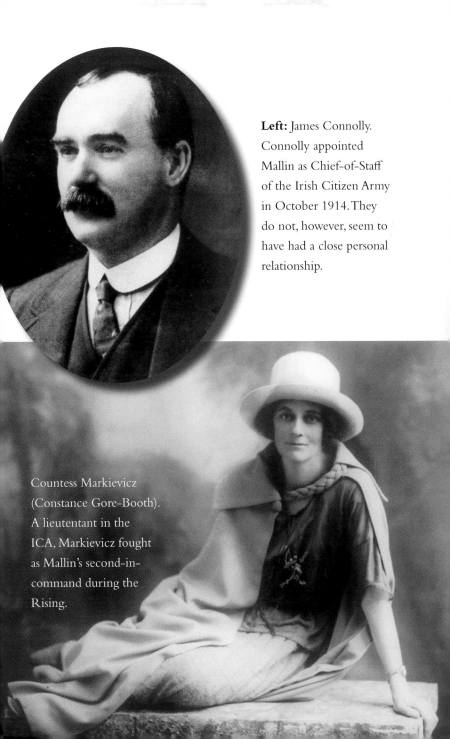

Left: James Connolly. Connolly appointed Mallin as Chief-of-Staff of the Irish Citizen Army in October 1914. They do not, however, seem to have had a close personal relationship.

Countess Markievicz (Constance Gore-Booth). A lieutentant in the ICA, Markievicz fought as Mallin's second-in-command during the Rising.

Left: 'Reasons to Join the Irish Citizen Army'. It is unclear when Mallin joined the ICA, but he does not seem to have been a member when the body was first formed.

Below: Liberty Hall in 1914. The *Irish Times* referred to the ITGWU headquarters as the centre of all social anarchy in Dublin.

HEAD OFFICE. IRISH TRANSPORT AND GENERAL WORKERS' UNION

Above: St Stephen's Green (view from the Royal College of Surgeons).
Mallin's troops abandoned Stephen's Green on Tuesday of Easter Week
and occupied the college.

Below: The Royal College of Surgeons: the college was solidly built
but of little strategic importance. Bullet holes are still visible in the
college facade.

Left: Mallin and his ICA comrades constructed barricades at intervals around Stephen's Green. Any cars that drove towards them soon ended up becoming part of the barricade.

Right: A receipt issued by the rebels for goods commandeered from grocer Alex Findlater during the Rising.

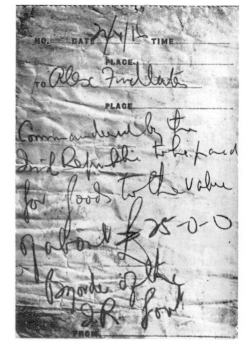

Theatre repertoire were performed alongside those such as *Under Which Flag?*, written by James Connolly. Mallin organised an orchestra of four to play at these events. One of the players, James Geoghegan, was killed in 1916.[22] The last of these concerts was held in Liberty Hall on Easter Sunday, 1916.

Mallin was particularly active at this time in trying to secure arms for the ICA. His family home at Emmet Hall in Inchicore was adjacent to Richmond barracks and Mallin was often in contact with 'friendly' soldiers who could obtain arms. The wall at the back of the premises was also part of the barracks and Mallin spent much time at the wall attempting to secure rifles. James O'Shea remembers spending many evenings under the barracks wall waiting for arms to be handed over. At one point there was a young English soldier willing to find them a machine gun but this did not work out. O'Shea related how he went to Mallin's house one evening and was told to wait. O'Shea knew Mallin was in the back garden looking for rifles and became more and more anxious as time wore on. Upon hearing a crash, O'Shea grabbed Mallin's sword and ran to the back wall and 'was about half way when I and my sword went up and down with a crash. I had fallen over something … It was poor Mallin!' He had been hit over the head by something thrown from the barracks and knocked unconscious, an attempt, O'Shea believed, to 'put him out for good.'[23] Séamus Mallin remembers three men confronting his father on the street on a separate occasion while he walked home one night. It is unclear whether the two attacks were related, but Mallin was apparently able to beat off his three attackers; two were left on the pavement and a third fled. The motive for this attack is unclear.[24] Maeve Cavanagh, who contributed poetry to the *Workers' Republic*, has noted how 'Mallin used to come a lot to our house. He was always collecting rifles and he told me he got a lot from the soldiers in Inchicore barracks and he often came in exhausted after these expeditions, and my sister used to make him a meal.' Mallin even managed to secure Cavanagh a .22mm revolver and ammunition.[25]

One aspect of Mallin's character that is consistently obvious during his time as Chief-of-Staff of the ICA is his insistence on discipline. It is not surprising that a man who had spent as long as Mallin in the British army would pick up a strong sense of discipline. During the silk weavers' strike in 1913, Mallin's reaction to the men who broke the strike some eleven weeks in is evidence of his demanding nature. This is again evident during his time in the ICA. James O'Shea's remarked that 'when Michael Mallin left an order … it was to be obeyed to the letter.'[26] Frank Robbins has described how:

> In the Citizen Army a higher degree of discipline was expected. It had been impressed on our minds by Commandant Mallin that the professional soldier carried out

orders because he knew the punishment that would await if he failed to do so, but Mallin emphasised time after time that he expected from us a discipline of a much higher degree, given freely because it was the right thing to do and not from any fear of punishment.[27]

That Mallin would emphasise this difference is revealing. At different stages of his life Mallin himself embodied both the career soldier and the volunteer, acting according to what he believed was 'the right thing to do'. It was in this latter position that Mallin would follow the path to insurrection.

The Worker's Republic

On 29 May 1915 a new version of James Connolly's newspaper the *Workers' Republic* appeared. The first edition contained a column entitled 'Irish Citizen Army', listing James Connolly as Commandant and Mallin as Chief-of-Staff. This column was continued in subsequent editions. The first article stated, 'We propose to give, under this heading, from time to time accounts of such military happenings in the past as may serve to enlighten and instruct our members.' The purpose of these articles was to 'discuss their achievements from the standpoint of their value to those who desire to see perfected a Citizen Army able to perform whatever duty may be thrust upon it.'[28] James Connolly wrote many of these articles himself, the first dealing with the Moscow Insurrection of 1905. After August 1915 Michael Mallin took over and wrote a number of articles, the first appearing on 7 August. These articles continued in much the same vein as Connolly's, pointing out lessons that could be learned from successful guerrilla operations. Mallin, though, had been a participant and a witness to the conflicts he wrote about; each article refers to guerrilla warfare in India during the period he was stationed there with the British army. The first referred to an engagement in June 1898 between the British army and an Indian tribe who had resented the imposition of a tax on them by the British. The British troops were camped outside a main village where they were attacked by the tribesmen. According to Mallin, the British spotted what they believed to be an attempted attack and changed the direction of their guns. This was, in fact, the old men, boys and women of the village who were used to trick the British – 'the ruse succeeded'. The armed men of the tribe were hidden in a number of dried up waterways or 'nullahs'. Mallin points out that 'To the tribesmen knowing every foot of the ground these nullahs were of the greatest assistance; to the troops who were strangers in the country … they were to the last degree dangerous.' The well-positioned tribe were able to ambush the British, inflict serious casualties and, according to Mallin, 'The retreat became a headlong panic-stricken flight, and thus ended the attempt to collect taxes by force.'[29]

Mallin's next article appeared on 28 August 1915 and

examined a conflict between another tribe, the 'Zakka Kels', and British forces in 1899. The conflict was the result of British attempts to capture the tribe's herd of cattle. The British General Officer Commanding, Mallin sarcastically wrote, 'conceived the very brilliant idea of seizing the cattle of those people to bring them to their senses, as it was called, through the hunger of their wives and children.' On marching to take the cattle the British forces encountered irregular and winding watercourses and hills, making the passing extremely dangerous. Mallin notes how as the commander advanced 'a well-directed fire was opened on his force by well-concealed marksmen.' The British troops were forced into retreat and as they fled 'groups of swordsmen, cunningly hidden and cleverly handled came into play.' These swordsmen waited until the enemy got close enough, and then proceeded to 'slash right through and away, disappearing round a further bend.' The British forces were defeated and the attempt to capture the cattle failed.[30]

In October 1915 two further articles penned by Mallin appeared dealing with a conflict at Samana Range in India in 1898. The conflict was between a tribe 'of Persian origin', who refused to agree with the British Indian government, and the British forces, upon whose flanks the tribe were encroaching. Mallin notes, significantly, that the tribe were 'armed, of course, as they always are, as freemen should be.' The area contained a number of small villages in which the fighting took place. Mallin describes how the tribe's force consisted of riflemen and swordsmen who took up positions in houses and at crossings. As the British forces entered the village the riflemen would fire to halt the advance and the swordsmen would then 'cut and hack' before escaping down a narrow passage. When the British eventually took the first village 'no one was found in it, with the possible exception of a few dogs, and even they were not friendly.' The whole tribe had moved on to another village.[31] The tribesmen soon launched a full attack on the British troops. As the British retreated, the boys of the village burnt large areas of grass, cutting off their escape route. Although the commanding officer was able to fight through, the escape came with 'very heavy losses.'[32]

A common theme emerges in Mallin's analysis of these conflicts that is also reflected in the other articles in the 'Irish Citizen Army' column: they deal with successful guerrilla operations of small, often poorly equipped groups against the superior firepower of the British army. This is the type of battle in which Connolly and Mallin envisaged the ICA to be engaged. As such, Mallin often acknowledges the crucial role of a good plan and good leadership. In one article, he writes of the tribesmen: 'the dispositions and handling generally of their fighting men would point to a well worked out plan, that plan being followed out to the end.'[33] He consistently highlights the good positions of marksmen and

rifles as crucial to the tribes' success. The use of the landscape
to the advantage of the tribes is repeatedly emphasised. Mallin
compares the irregular, uneven landscape of India with its
systems of dried up rivers, or 'nullahs', to the narrow streets
and lanes leading from larger main streets in an urban setting.
The tribesmen used this landscape to their advantage, firing
on the enemy until they got too close and then retreating
down the smaller nullahs. Mallin points to the effectiveness
of this tactic in street fighting: 'You can understand twenty
or thirty men defending a barricade in a main street, and on
the troops pressing them too closely retiring down one of the
side streets ... To parties defending their own cities in such a
manner the lanes and side streets are of incalculable value.'[34]
The close-quarters attacks from swordsmen are also shown
to have inflicted severe casualties and Mallin is keen to point
out the danger of small side streets and lanes to regular troops.

Similarly, Mallin highlights the use of delaying tactics
by these tribes. In Samana Range he believes the people
'fought a delaying fight with of course the possible chance
of a victory.' He points out that in a revolutionary movement, 'Delaying fights are one of the first things aimed at.
The Revolutionaries may and will have to take up positions
in parts of a city to delay troops for the necessary length
of time required for the leaders to formulate their plans',
further noting that a 'delay of one half hour may mean the
winning for his side.'[35]

These comments are most valuable for what they tell us about Mallin's military thinking. One comment that bears particular resonance to Mallin's tactics during the Rising – it is, after all, Mallin's commanding of rebels for which he is remembered – came in the article published on 9 October. While defending a small village the men 'put it in a state of defence by digging deep and very wide trenches about midway down the streets or passages. They were too wide for the troops to jump across.'[36] When Mallin's garrison entered St Stephen's Green on Easter Monday, Mallin ordered the men to dig trenches to defend the area. This has been roundly criticised by historians. The success of the tactic in India as described by Mallin perhaps offers some insight into Mallin's mindset on Easter Monday. Did Mallin apply a tactic he had seen work well many years previously to the unfamiliar situation in which he found himself on the first day of the rebellion? The trench warfare that characterised the western front during World War I, still raging in April 1916, would also have been fresh in the mind and offers another compelling point of comparison.

However, what is most striking about Mallin's writing in the *Worker's Republic* is how little resemblance the tactics of the Indian tribes bear to the events of Easter Week, in Mallin's garrison or elsewhere in the city (except, perhaps, Mount Street Bridge and Northumberland Road). The articles were published to educate ICA members and to prepare them for the warfare in which they were soon to be engaged. As it turned out, very little of what the men read in these articles was of any use to those who found themselves facing machine-gun fire from a pit or hemmed inside a large building awaiting attack.

As Mallin was stationed with the British army in India for these conflicts it is worth noting his attitude towards the British army as it appears in these articles, written many years later. For example, Mallin is not overly critical of the officers in charge of the British troops. Regarding Samana Range, he claims that, 'Only for the steady, cool manner in which this Commanding Officer handled his force in the face of the terrible situation … he would have lost every man without question.'[37] It is the motivation of the British army behind these engagements that Mallin is more critical of – the imposition of a tax by force and an attempt to capture cattle. He describes the Tirah campaign as 'very unprofitable'.[38] It is, perhaps, not a surprise to find here a former soldier who, despite a moral disagreement with the war he was forced to fight, retains a loyalty and respect for those he fought alongside. Importantly, we also see an element of Mallin's character that is crucial when attempting to understand his decision to participate in a rebellion: a sympathy for and understanding of the rights and dignity of the poor. Mallin displays a strong understanding of the social standing of the native population in India and is clearly aware of the consequences the British campaign could have on their standard of living. His sympathies are clear. He shows an understanding of the 'system of control or management' of the small villages in the region, indicating empathy not always associated with soldiers of occupation.[39] Mallin's description of the fighting in Samana Range ends on a poignant note:

> No one in this country knows anything about the horrors that column went through, there was no such thing as surrender. The tribesmen of Tirah asked for no quarter and gave none. The General Officer Commanding (General Lockhart) became insane shortly after we got back to India.[40]

The 'we' here is the only direct reference to Mallin's own involvement in the events he has described.

One remarkable development arose from these articles, according to James O'Shea. O'Shea claims that Mallin was taken by a government official one evening to meet a judge. The judge told Mallin that 'the Government was annoyed with him, he who had a military training and was so long in the British army ... They had read his articles in *Worker* and were delighted at his military intelligence and tactics.' Mallin was then apparently asked to take up a commission in the army which he, unsurprisingly, refused. This, according to O'Shea, was followed by a meeting with a friend of Mallin's from the Royal Scots Fusiliers, who 'was on an official visit from Scotland by order of the War Office to get him to give up his rebel activities and join his Regiment.' Mallin again refused.[41] If this did happen it was probably in early 1916 – O'Shea claims it was about five weeks before the attack at the wall of Richmond barracks, which he believes was linked to the meetings. The veracity of O'Shea's story is impossible to confirm. If, however, O'Shea's comments are to be believed they suggest a wider appreciation of Mallin's military ability than has been previously acknowledged. It would also suggest that Mallin's military thinking was believed to be of a high standard. This is significant when compared to the later criticism of Mallin's tactics during the Easter Rising.

James Connolly's 'Disappearance'

The Supreme Council of the Irish Republican Brotherhood (IRB), a secret society determined to obtain Irish independence from Britain by the use of force, met soon after the outbreak of the Great War in 1914 and decided to launch a rebellion at some time in the future. A small 'advisory committee' was established to formulate a plan; no records of its plan remain nor was it shown to the Supreme Council. In May 1915 a 'military committee' (which later became known as the 'military council') was formed. Initially there were three members – Patrick Pearse, Éamonn Ceannt and Joseph Plunkett. In September they were joined by the driving force behind the plans for insurrection: Thomas Clarke and Seán MacDiarmada. Their plan was to use the rank and file of the Irish Volunteers – those who had decided not to follow John Redmond's call to fight in the Great War – to launch a rebellion while the British were considerably stretched by the demands of the war. The IRB were worried, however, by the increasingly militant rhetoric of ICA leader James Connolly. Fearing the ICA would start a rebellion alone and scupper their own plans, the IRB resolved to get Connolly on-side.

On Wednesday, 19 January 1916, James Connolly left Liberty Hall at lunchtime and was not to return until 22 January. Exactly what happened during the days of Connolly's 'disappearance' has never been satisfactorily confirmed. What is certain is that by the time he returned, Connolly had agreed that the ICA would join the Irish Volunteers in an insurrection and he had been co-opted onto the military council of the IRB. Thomas MacDonagh was also co-opted, bringing the number to seven.

As Connolly's second-in-command, this was significant for Michael Mallin as it paved his path towards rebellion, but contemporary accounts also indicate that Mallin played his own role in the events. William O'Brien, a labour leader and trade union official, was told by Countess Markievicz that Connolly, Mallin and herself had an arrangement that if any of them were to be arrested the ICA would start an insurrection on its own. Markievicz had been an honorary treasurer of the ICA since its foundation and was often seen at the head of route marches with the men. O'Brien recalls that when a telegram, addressed from Lucan, which they believed to be from Connolly was received, Dr Kathleen Lynn (the ICA medical officer) 'drove Helena Maloney, Commandant Mallin's wife who was a native of Lucan, and myself to Lucan on Friday evening.' They were unable to prove the telegram was from Connolly[42] (Liam Ó Briain, an Irish Volunteer who fought under Mallin during the Rising, claims he was told that Connolly was kept in Lucan during this time.[43]). According to William O'Brien, Countess Markievicz was eager for the ICA to mobilise and complained about being 'held back'. She was convinced by O'Brien and Mallin to wait and mobilise only if Connolly had not returned by Monday.[44] Connolly, in fact, returned on Saturday evening.

According to a number of accounts it seems that Mallin played a significant role in Connolly's 'release', visiting the military council of the IRB to demand the release of Connolly. Frank Robbins describes a conversation he had with Mallin about this event: Mallin, he relates, said that he had told the meeting that if they did not release Connolly before a certain time the ICA would take action. When Éamonn Ceannt sarcastically remarked, 'What could your small number do in such a situation?' Mallin replied, 'We can fight and we can die, and it will be to our glory and your shame if such does take place.' Patrick Pearse then banged on the table and said, 'Yes, by God, that is so, and here is one who is with you.'[45] While Robbins may have provided a somewhat glossy version of the events, there may well be at least some truth in his account. Liam Ó Briain's recollection of a conversation with Mallin in Richmond barracks after the collapse of the Rising is very similar to Robbins's. In Ó Briain's version, Mallin approached the Volunteer leaders, informed them of the Citizen Army's pact to begin an insurrection if Connolly were to go missing and stated that he himself and Markievicz would begin the fight on the following Saturday, adding that 'the Volunteers could join them or not, as they liked.'[46] James O'Shea has recalled how '[Mallin] got a move on it and told headquarters staff of Volunteers who had kidnapped him if he was not home at a given time he would attack Dublin Castle … Mallin told me he got the best of the bargain as he held them to certain dates.'[47]

Diarmuid Lynch, an active member of the IRB, has expressed serious reservations about this meeting as it appeared in Fox's *History of the Irish Citizen Army*. Firstly, he is doubtful that all the members of the IRB military council were at the meeting (Mallin was apparently unaware of the existence of a military council, probably believing he was attending a meeting of leaders of the Irish Volunteers – Ó Briain and O'Shea both refer to the Volunteer leadership). Lynch believes the Pearse comment to be a 'fabrication' and

writes: 'Was Pearse "with" Mallin in this? *I do not believe it
– not for one moment.*'[48] Moreover, Lynch is convinced
that it was not Mallin's intrusion that facilitated Connolly's
release, but rather Connolly's agreement to act with the
military council:

> Had he not acquiesced, does anyone believe they would
> have released him? And in the event of his continued cus-
> tody, who is so naïve as to believe that Mallin would have
> been permitted to remain at large to lead the I.C.A. into
> immediate action? ... [They] would have found a way to
> deal with Mallin.[49]

As an IRB member himself, Lynch's comments are not
surprising. These comments all imply that Connolly was
'kidnapped' by the IRB leadership and released only when
he had agreed to act alongside them. It is not, in fact, certain that Connolly was kidnapped at all, and if he was, by
whom. Whether it was the case in reality or not, Mallin
probably believed Connolly had been kidnapped (he seems
to have said little himself to clear up the matter) and that
his own ultimatum had forced Connolly's release.

Notwithstanding the disputed versions of events, after
his disappearance Connolly became an influential contributor to the planned insurrection. With Connolly on
board, Mallin and the ICA would become immersed in the
plans for, and execution of, the Easter Rising. James O'Shea

noted a more friendly relationship between the ICA and the Volunteers from this date; Mallin and Connolly began lecturing Volunteers on street fighting.[50] From that point on, they prepared for war.

Chapter 7

1916
The Eve of the Revolution

The plan for insurrection was shrouded in secrecy. Spies and informers had been the curse of previous generations of rebels; it was the information of spies that condemned Thomas Clarke to fifteen years in the English prison system. The plan to counteract this was a simple one: the Irish Volunteers were to be mobilised on Easter Sunday 1916, but not told what for. Once out, they would be led into battle. When Connolly became a member of the military council the Irish Citizen Army were destined to join the Volunteers in the rebellion. The Citizen Army was given its own orders by Connolly for Easter Sunday – to parade at Liberty Hall in full uniform at 3.30pm – to tie in with the Volunteers' plans. While the desire for action caused a distinctive split among Volunteer and IRB hierarchy, the ICA leadership were united in the belief that the Citizen Army would fight soon, alone if necessary. High-ranking members of the IRB and Volunteers who were opposed to an unprovoked rebellion, Chief-of-Staff Eoin MacNeill included, were kept aloof of the plans while the military council plotted. In the months preceding the Rising, Irish Volunteer officers were lectured on various aspects of insurrection and urban warfare (including lectures from Connolly and Mallin). These lectures were aimed to 'attune their minds to participation in an insurrection' as well as to instruct. Volunteers were regularly warned by their superiors that they would be called into action soon.[1]

Among many Volunteers, there was an explicit feeling that something big was coming, but no great sense of what or when. The rank and file of the Citizen Army, on the other hand, seem to have had a much clearer idea of the plans for insurrection. In 1915 all members had been brought to James Connolly and individually asked three questions: Are you prepared to take part in the fight for Ireland's freedom? Are you prepared to fight alongside the Irish Volunteers? Are you prepared to fight without the aid of the Irish Volunteers or any other allies?[2] As the proposed date approached, the upcoming insurrection was spoken of openly in Citizen Army circles: 'This was not hidden or spoken of with bated breath,' insisted ICA member James O'Shea. 'We all knew and discussed openly our aims and objects and we told everybody what we were drilling for.'[3]

Nellie Donnelly (*née* Gifford) ran a small public employment bureau in Harcourt Street in 1916. Donnelly remembers that about a month before the Rising, Mallin entered her bureau and announced the plans for an insurrection, stating, 'It is all fixed now'. Mallin told Donnelly that the Rising was arranged for Easter Sunday.[4] Frank Robbins was one of a number of officers who were called in to James Connolly on Spy Wednesday when, in Mallin's presence, they were each told exactly what their role would be in the first stages of the fight. Thomas O'Donoghue also recalls attending this meeting, although he is less clear on the date.[5] On Good Friday morning James O'Shea was told by Mallin that the fight might begin at any time and he was advised not to return to work until he received further orders. That evening Connolly issued mobilisation orders for the Citizen Army as well as officers' commissions which were to come into effect as soon as the rebellion began. Mallin was given the rank of commandant.[6]

A week earlier, the DMP had raided Liberty Hall to seize copies of the *The Gael* newspaper. They were confronted and threatened by an armed James Connolly before making a hasty retreat. Immediately afterwards, a mobilisation order was issued by Connolly to all ICA members, delivered to Mallin by Christopher Brady (who later gained fame as one of the printers of the Proclamation), and from then there was a constant armed guard at Liberty Hall. Liam Ó Briain, a member of the 3rd Dublin brigade of the Irish Volunteers who jumped the railing to join the Stephen's Green garrison on Easter Monday, was struck by how much ICA members knew in advance of the Rising. To Ó Briain they 'seemed to have known all about it for a fortnight or so beforehand, and to have been working day and night in preparation.'[7]

In the days leading up to the outbreak of the rebellion, Liberty Hall was awash with activity. James O'Shea has recalled how it felt to be an ICA member in Liberty Hall at this time:

> Liberty Hall at this period was peculiar. As a member of the Citizen Army you felt strange when out of it and each man of the army lived most of the time with his rifle and bayonet. In fact, they seemed to become as much a part of him as his trousers. You saw men polishing and oiling rifles as if their lives depended on it. No man had to be urged to do anything. It was a matter of trying to outdo one another for guards, dangerous jobs etc., goings and comings. Strange faces of Volunteer officers passed you on the stairs asking for James Connolly and admiring our guard system.[8]

A team of men under Captain McGowan spent the weekend industriously making bombs and other munitions. Female members prepared food, rations and medical supplies. On Good Friday a young ICA member, William Oman, was sent by Mallin to Amiens Street to report on any movements

of police or troops. There he noticed James Connolly entering Houlihan's basket maker's, shortly followed by Patrick
Pearse and Seán MacDiarmada. Later he reported what he
had seen to Mallin who informed him that it was a meeting of the 'Provisional Government'. Mallin then told Oman
that the *Aud* had sunk, before adding, 'I don't know where
we go from here.'[9] That evening the military council had
been informed of the arrest of Roger Casement, who had
travelled to the Kerry coast in a German submarine, and
the scuttling of the steamship, the *Aud*, in Cork harbour –
the *Aud* had been carrying German rifles and ammunition,
organised by Casement, for use in the rebellion and had been
due to meet with Casement to hand over its cargo. A series
of misunderstandings and misfortunes meant the handover
never took place and the ship was scuttled by its crew after
an attempt to return home was blocked by British ships.

The same day, another disaster befell the Rising's planners.
Eoin MacNeill was opposed to a rising without provocation
and a clear chance of success and had only agreed to the
insurrection when he believed the British authorities were
planning a large-scale round-up of the Volunteers and other
nationalist organisations. When MacNeill discovered he
had been misled, he immediately cancelled the manoeuvres
planned for Sunday and in doing so crushed any chances of a
mass mobilisation in Dublin and a rising around the country.
MacNeill's countermanding order was distributed around

the country by messengers and published in the *Sunday Independent*. Learning of MacNeill's cancellation, but unaffected by the order, the ICA embarked on a route march on Sunday afternoon, led by Mallin and a furious James Connolly. R.M. Fox has described this route march:

> At about 4 pm, they set out headed by a band. Each man was fully equipped for the fight. They marched across Butt Bridge, along to College Green, Grafton Street, down York Street, along George's Street and the centre of the city. Every man was tensed up and prepared for action. If there had been any interference by police or soldiers, they were ready to start the fight. But there was no movement from the other side. Back they marched to Liberty Hall, where tea was served ... The route march served the double purpose of giving the men something to do and taking the attention of the growing crowd off Liberty Hall.

That morning, the military council had met and decided to postpone the Rising until the following morning, Easter Monday. Around the same time, while on his way to Liberty Hall, James O'Shea met Agnes Mallin and her four children – James, John, Una and Joseph – on the quays close to O'Connell bridge. Agnes looked 'pale and anxious but quite calm' and O'Shea 'admired her courage'. Recognising the significance of what was to come he offered to bring them to Mallin ('She knew all. I was sorry for the kids, so young and not knowing what was going on'). He brought the family into Liberty Hall and left them alone with Mallin. When O'Shea next saw Mallin they had left.[10]

With the Rising confirmed to begin the next morning, most of the ICA members spent the night in Liberty Hall. That evening they held an improvised concert given by Mallin's four-piece Worker's Orchestra and Mallin played the flute.[11] 'On the eve of the revolution,' remembered the pianist, 'we set to our task as usual and played all the night as if it were just a normal night.'[12] Whatever trepidation those in Liberty Hall may have felt, it was not evident as they bedded down. Bernie Craven, a bald Dublin cabby, became the subject of mockery ('it was a good omen for the fight to see two moons shining together') and Craven's attempts to remonstrate met with further laughter as did his 'sermon on death which caused more sport up to 12 o'clock when someone came in and put us to silence.'

The men had been ordered to proceed immediately to the windows of the building upon hearing a whistle; at about 1.30am the whistle sounded and in his haste to get to the window James O'Shea forgot his trousers: 'This caused a great laugh ... during this terrible time there was always time for a laugh.'[13] Later, the men were counted by Mallin and Captain Seán Connolly (no relation of James) and Mallin read out a list of names of those who were detailed to take City Hall under Captain Connolly's command. O'Shea recalls the strong impression made on him by both men at this time. Seán Connolly was 'great looking in full uniform. He was as brave looking as if he was Robert Emmet.' Mallin 'was dead cool. His speech was to the point and no word wasted. He was the practical soldier all the time.'[14]

Chapter 8

• • • • •

1916
Easter Week

At 9.00am on Easter Monday morning, 24 April 1916, Thomas O'Donoghue, taking up his commission as an ICA lieutenant, was ordered by Mallin to post guards and take charge of the defence of Liberty Hall. Most Citizen Army members had spent the night in Liberty Hall, but those who had been granted passes to go home for the night filed back during the morning. They were joined by Irish Volunteers and the members of the IRB military council. At 10.00am Mallin, expecting perhaps to lead the ICA in the fight alone and clearly pessimistic about what was to come, commented to James O'Shea: 'We will be fighting in a short time and we may have to fight alone ... It will be short and sharp ... We will all be dead in a short time.'[1] O'Shea has described how he felt while waiting to set out:

... we each had our own thoughts and little things that never mattered before came into our minds. Home, people, friends and the chances of the fight, what it would be like being killed, what of the next world. These remote things that never gave you a thought before seemed important at the moment. It did not fill you with sorrow or foreboding, only a kind of abstract removal from realities.[2]

By 11.45am O'Donoghue and the other ICA officers had been instructed to inform the men to fall in. Mallin then appointed to each officer the men under their command. As they marched off to their positions, O'Donoghue asked Mallin if they were marching into the fight, to which Mallin replied, 'Yes, we are out.'[3] They marched in the brilliant sunshine from Liberty Hall and down Aston Quay. Frank Robbins recalls the clock on the Ballast Office on the corner of Westmoreland Street and Aston Quay reading 11.55am and a rush – some men almost running – through Westmoreland Street and Grafton Street as they strove to reach their destination by noon. A young DMP officer, irritated by their singing of 'The Peeler and the Goat', briefly confronted them, but otherwise the march passed without incident.[4] James O'Shea remembers taking a different route (an unsurprising discrepancy, perhaps, given the pace at which events were moving) across Butt bridge, down Tara Street and towards College Green. As they marched, O'Shea thought about those who were at that moment travelling to the seaside, countryside or Fairyhouse races and 'smiled to think that at 12 o'clock noon, a matter of minutes, we would be fighting for our lives and our country.'[5]

Though no detailed records survive, it seems the original plan for the Rising envisaged a general uprising in both Dublin and the provinces and allowed for a westward retreat if they were unable to hold the capital. The loss of the *Aud* and MacNeill's countermanding order seriously undermined this plan. Though still unlikely to end in victory, the intended rising was to bring out a far more formidable military force than the rising that actually took place. By committing to a smaller rebellion confined to the centre of the city, the leaders completely abandoned any real hope of a military success.

Taking the British administration and the Dublin Metropolitan Police by surprise, the rebels were able to occupy and clear these posts with little resistance or difficulty. The rebels occupied a number of sites around the capital. The General Post Office (GPO) became headquarters and also taken were Boland's mills, Jacob's biscuit factory, the South Dublin Union, the Four Courts, the Mendicity Institute and St Stephen's Green. At noon Patrick Pearse read the Proclamation of the Irish Republic from the front of the GPO to a largely indifferent audience. Five of the seven men who had signed the Proclamation – Patrick Pearse, James Connolly, Thomas Clarke, Seán MacDiarmada and Joseph Plunkett – were based in the GPO. Pearse assumed the role of President of the Irish Republic and Commander-in-Chief of the republican forces. James Connolly served as Commandant-General of the forces in Dublin. Though Connolly was tasked with controlling all the rebel forces in Dublin, in practice the rebel posts outside the GPO had to rely on their own devices. The other two signatories of the Proclamation, Thomas MacDonagh and Éamonn Ceannt, commanded the rebels in Jacob's biscuit factory and the South Dublin Union respectively. Éamon de Valera occupied Boland's mills with his force, while Edward Daly did likewise at the Four Courts. Seán Heuston, following orders from James Connolly, marched a group of fourteen men from Mountjoy Square to the Mendicity Institute and Con Colbert first occupied Watkins' brewery before later moving to the Jameson distillery on Marrowbone Lane.

The men under Michael Mallin's command were assigned to take Stephen's Green, a large, enclosed public park about a mile south of the General Post Office and a short distance from Jacob's biscuit factory. The park was made up of some twenty acres of open space containing a bandstand, summerhouse and ornamental lake and surrounded by a number of tall buildings on each side, the most prominent of which was the Shelbourne Hotel to the north. Stephen's Green and the surrounding area was a significant transport centre for the south-eastern side of the city and, in that sense, strategically important. Despite the disruption brought about by the cancellation of the previous day's orders, an impressive 219 men and women turned out for the ICA on Monday morning, almost two-thirds of those who had previously told Connolly they were willing to fight. The ICA turnout, proportionally higher than that of the Irish Volunteers, had much to do with the greater militancy and undivided leadership of the body.

As the main body under ICA command was reaching Stephen's Green, a small section under Séan Connolly reached their position in the vicinity of City Hall. As Connolly approached the main gate of Dublin Castle, the symbolic seat of British administration in Ireland, he fired what were the first shots of the Rising, simultaneously claiming the first victim, the unarmed DMP constable James O'Brien. They tied up the six sentries on duty in the castle guardroom. Major A.J. Price, chief intelligence officer of the British army, upon hearing shots fired, rushed to the castle yard and began firing from his revolver before wisely retreating. Connolly's men, mysteriously, did likewise and entered City Hall next door. Their actions in these early moments of revolution and the surprising decision not to attempt to take Dublin Castle, despite its weak defences, has been the subject of much historical discussion, but Seán Connolly would be dead within an hour, shot on the roof of City Hall, the first insurgent casualty.

Another company of ICA men headed for the Harcourt

Street railway station, with a detachment of seven men under Sergeant Doyle moving to occupy Davy's public house on Portobello bridge. Frank Robbins has described the scene in the station:

> An order was issued to the general public to leave the foyer and get up on the platform. We then announced that the Irish Republic had been declared ... This caused consternation among the many holiday trippers, including women and children, who became very frightened ... a number of men inside the ticket office ... had locked the door against our men ... a revolver shot into the lock had the effect of convincing the men inside of our determination.[6]

Soon the station was cleared and all those inside were gathered on the platform. However, an attempt to use an engine to block the railway line failed as the signalman locked the points, the officer in command being unable to prevent this act of defiance. Robbins's excuse was a lack of manpower.[7] This was to be a recurring complaint from those who survived the fighting. With the station taken, Robbins and two others then took to their own assignment: the building of barricades at both ends of Hatch Street, presumably to protect the southern end of the Green. As the Easter bank holiday meant an absence of cabs and hackney cars, Robbins was forced to commandeer motor cars for the barricade from a garage on Earlsfort Terrace. With the barricades in place,

Robbins and his men, in line with orders, retreated to Stephen's Green and the main ICA contingent.[8] The men who occupied Davy's public house also fell back to the Green after a short gunfight.

Upon entering Stephen's Green, the main body of men under Mallin's command set about clearing the park of bystanders and securing their position. When the park was cleared, the gates were shut, armed men were placed along the railings on the north side and entrances were barricaded. Mallin's headquarters were established in a kiosk and a summer-house was improvised as a kitchen. A first-aid centre was established and run by Madeleine ffrench-Mullen. Arms and ammunition were distributed by cart around the green and the men began the work of digging trenches and rifle pits.[9] Soon after the Green was occupied, Countess Markievicz (who held the ICA rank of lieutenant) was appointed as Mallin's second-in-command. According to the ICA's medical officer Dr Kathleen Lynn, Markievicz, who had been in Lynn's car distributing medical supplies, had intended to travel back and forth to all the rebel posts but only made it as far as Stephen's Green. By Lynn's account, Mallin asked her to stay, first as a sniper but soon appointing her as his second-in-command. Markievicz's role in the Rising quickly became the stuff of folklore. Her enthusiastic approach to her new role, her distinctive dress (an old Citizen Army tunic of Mallin's, puttees, a hat complete with ostrich feather, and a revolver), and, indeed, her gender, meant she drew much attention from witnesses – many thought it was she who was in charge in Stephen's Green. Markievicz, though the most famous, was not the only late arrival on Monday; around twenty others, including Irish Volunteers Liam Ó Briain and Harry Nicholls, unable to meet up with their own companies, volunteered to throw in their lot with the men in Stephen's Green.[10] The garrison was further augmented on Tuesday by between fifteen and twenty reinforcements sent by Thomas MacDonagh from Jacob's biscuit factory.

As well as the digging of trenches, much of Monday was spent building barricades in the streets surrounding the Green. Barricades were formed with carts, cars, furniture and other large items that necessarily had to be commandeered from the general public, often to their considerable displeasure. One member of the garrison, Thomas O'Donoghue, commandeered a very 'fine-looking limousine' from a bewildered clergyman whom he took to be the Protestant Archbishop of Armagh.[11] Some members of the public bravely attempted to retrieve their commandeered possessions and had to be threatened and chased off at gunpoint.[12] Others displayed more resolve: Frank Robbins admired the bravery of a tram driver and his conductor who, despite having a warning shot fired in their direction, managed to drive their tram away from the rebels.[13] Commandeering material had mixed results, as emphasised in the diary of one bystander, Lily Stokes:

> Outside the Shelbourne they – the Volunteers – had a bar-
> ricade. As I was passing a splendid motor came whirling
> down the east side; it was instantly held up and ordered
> into the barricade. Out of it stepped a dignitary of the R.C.
> Church. The Volunteer saluted: 'I beg your pardon, My
> Lord, but it is my orders.' [This is probably the same inci-
> dent related by O'Donoghue.] In the barricade there was a
> big dray (its horse shot dead close by), a side car, two motors
> and a big laundry van, out of which baskets had fallen, their
> contents lying about. ...Another motor came flying into the
> trap, was held up and ordered in the same way. Its owner
> refused and backed the car, the Rebels following threaten-
> ing him with their guns. We all thought they would shoot
> him but they shot his tyres instead. An elderly gentleman
> beside me turned, and said: 'If those ruffians had shot him, I
> would have shot them', and showed me his revolver up his
> sleeve. I am glad he did not shoot for he would certainly
> have been shot himself.[14]

Not all of the barricades were adequately built to fulfil
their function either. At Stephen's Green's Harcourt Street
gate, cars returning from the Fairyhouse races were able
to pass through the barricade constructed there, under fire
from nearby trenches, as the day progressed.[15] Throughout
Monday the Green was surrounded by a large number of

curious spectators. A senior civil servant noticed a group of women who had 'come out to see the battle' sitting on chairs around Stephen's Green.[16] Some seemed to take it as a joke and showed little concern for any possible danger, one observer describing the scene at one of the gates into the Green:

> A man was standing inside the gates, holding a rifle and looking intently down Grafton Street. Some girls were chaffing him, and asking him if he was not scared to death, and what would his mother say if she could see him, and was he not afraid that she would give him a beating ... now and then, when someone obscured his vision of the street, he gruffly ordered them away, and if they did not move speedily, he threatened them, 'G'long with you!' they would say, still chaffing, but a little uncertain.[17]

Others were clearly hostile. The most vocal were the women from the tenements around Stephen's Green and the wives of men serving on the western front with the British army — the 'separation women'. During the week, on hearing a suggestion from a man to bury a dead rebel lying inside the Green, one woman 'rushed at him and beat him with her fists and swore at him horribly. "No, you'll not get him out," she yelled. "Let him lie there and rot, like the poor soldiers!"'[18]

There were a number of British soldiers around Stephen's

Green when the Rising broke out. Thomas O'Donoghue prevented Vincent Poole (himself a former British army soldier) from shooting an unarmed British officer. O'Donoghue released the officer on a promise that he would not divulge any information about their position or numbers.[19] In stark contrast to O'Donoghue's rather polite interaction, James O'Shea claims to have fired his shotgun through the park's railings at a British soldier in khaki who, pretending to be intoxicated, was using abusive language towards the garrison, referring to the female members as prostitutes. O'Shea was convinced he was there as a spy and, having shot him, ordered two witnesses, at gunpoint, to remove the body.[20] A number of other British servicemen were taken prisoner, at least for a short time, on Monday.

In general, there was relatively little bloodshed on the first day of the Rising, but Citizen Army men were involved in some contentious killings. DMP Constable Michael Lahiff was an early casualty of the occupation of Stephen's Green. Lahiff was shot three times in the head, allegedly by Markievicz, for refusing to leave his post in the Green.[21] Lahiff was unarmed. Confrontations with the civilians who had gathered to watch the fighting occasionally ended in violence. At Hatch Street a civilian was shot dead for refusing to help build a barricade and his companion was only saved from a similar fate by Frank Robbins's intervention.[22] One of the most infamous civilian casualties of the Rising was an elderly gentleman, Michael Cavanagh, a guest in the Shelbourne Hotel. His shooting was witnessed by the author James Stephens. According to his eye-witness account, Cavanagh's cart of theatrical props had been commandeered and when Cavanagh attempted to reclaim the cart he was told by the men in the Green to leave it where it was. Three warning shots were fired before Cavanagh dropped the handles of the cart and approached the men behind the railings. He was shot in the head.[23] W.G. Smith, an ambulance driver who came to Stephen's Green to see what was happening, also witnessed the shooting. He described the effect on the crowd: 'Women began to shriek & cry & kneel down and to pray in the street.' Some of the female members of the garrison seem to have been equally affected and 'began crying & screaming & wringing their hands, to be told by the rebels to go home & several of them were sent off.'[24]

There were also some lucky escapes during the opening moments of the insurrection. Richard McCormick was only prevented from making an unarmed DMP officer on Harcourt Street his 'first job' of the Rising by Thomas MacDonagh's request not to have unnecessary bloodshed. In Harcourt Street station Frank Robbins came close to shooting a holidaying British army officer and Michael Donnelly shot the hat from the head of a gentleman who attempted to disarm one of his colleagues.[25] Those stationed in Stephen's Green were ordered not to fire until they heard firing from Harcourt

Street. As soon as the men in the Green were allowed to return fire, James O'Shea, who seems to have been particularly eager to do as much shooting as possible, ran to the railings to take aim at a policeman who had made sarcastic remarks as the garrison were marching. O'Shea claims he later shot the cap off a British army officer who was travelling by in a motor car.[26]

Some of this early ill-discipline is perhaps due to the excitement of the first moments of rebellion and the over-exuberance of youth. Those who fought during Easter Week were generally younger men and women. There were a number of young members of the ICA who took part in the fighting, but others seem to have come along after the outbreak of the Rising. Mallin's small garrison appears to have been augmented by a large number of excitable youngsters. James O'Shea took in a seventeen-year-old, keen to join the fight, and instructed him in the use of a shotgun and grenades.[27] A civilian, Diarmuid Coffey, wandered onto Stephen's Green on Monday and noted how young some of the participants were: 'Many of those in the Green were mere boys and there were a few girls, one of whom was distributing oranges to the boys.' Similarly, to W.G. Smith's eyes, 'Many of them were mere boys; in fact only about one in ten was a man; they had a great many girls, ranging from about 13 to 20, furnished with haversacks acting as *vivandiers* to their army.' Many of these boys were allowed to perform a military role, perhaps another result of the shortage of manpower. Lily Stokes, a resident of Raglan Road, thought the trenches at the Green's gates 'were chiefly manned by children – lads of 16 or 17.'[28] According to Coffey, one young boy fired a shot without reason and was promptly ordered to stop by the others.[29]

Later on Monday a group under Frank Robbins, including Markievicz, was sent by Mallin to occupy the Royal College of Surgeons. The immediate purpose, according to Robbins, was to secure a number of service rifles and ammunition that they believed were stored in the building. In order to take the caretaker of the building by surprise, while he was remonstrating with a civilian at the main door, the group made it seem as if they were proceeding towards York Street before quickly dashing towards the door. A shot was fired and Robbins was able to jam his foot into the door to prevent the caretaker from closing it. With Robbins's gun pointed at his throat, the caretaker wisely stepped aside and spent the rebellion as a prisoner with his wife and son.[30]

Meanwhile, the majority of the garrison continued to dig themselves in. Harry Nicholls accompanied Mallin and Markievicz on a patrol, taking in Harcourt Street, Camden Street, moving down towards Jacob's biscuit factory and back to the Green via York Street.[31] Mallin and Markievicz spent much of Monday checking up on those under their command, all the while offering assurances that the fight was going well.

Mallin's garrison would have been, for the most part, totally unaware of what was going on in the other positions around the city, a situation that continued throughout the week. In general, rebels were reliant on their commanding officers for information about how the fight was going elsewhere. The main source of communication between the rebel bases was through dispatch riders, usually female, who delivered messages between the garrison leaders. No evidence survives of what was contained in many of these dispatches, but rank-and-file members were rarely, if ever, aware of the contents. It is also unclear exactly how much information was contained in dispatches received by Mallin and how much knowledge he had (or indeed, how accurate that knowledge was) of the situation around the city as the week progressed.

Several prisoners were taken during the occupation of Stephen's Green, including a number of British servicemen. The garrison also detained a British Red Cross worker whose skills would be useful.[32] One British soldier, relaxing in the park with his girlfriend, had quite an agreeable experience. He was taken prisoner in the bandstand, given tea and cucumber sandwiches and heard to remark that he hoped there would be a rebellion every day as the food was 'bloody lovely'.[33] Among the other captives was Laurence J. Kettle. Kettle was Chief Engineer of Dublin Corporation's Electricity Department and the brother of Thomas Kettle MP, a nationalist and poet who had joined the British army to fight in the First World War and was killed in action in September 1916. He had been seen entering a military barracks, probably to see his brother, and was therefore considered to be an important military prisoner. Frank Robbins recalls that in the College of Surgeons Kettle volunteered to help as the men made use of the college's substantial supply of books to barricade windows. When Robbins decided to take a rest in a chair in the college, Kettle advised him to move as he was in the line of sniper fire.[34] One British officer taken prisoner was given 'parole "as an officer and a gentleman" not to escape' and allowed to roam at large in the Green. Markievicz later claimed this prisoner, 'walked around, found out all he could and then "bunked".'[35] It seems that prisoners were generally well treated. Margaret Skinnider, a Glaswegian who had travelled to Ireland to take part in the Rising, has stated that the garrison's prisoners complimented them on following the rules of warfare.[36] Unlike Kettle who, on Connolly's orders, was kept until the end of the week, most of the garrison's prisoners were released early in the week as the rebels did not have enough manpower to keep them under guard.

ICA officer Robert de Coeur had been instructed by Mallin on Monday to lead a group to take a row of houses that ran down to Lower Leeson Street bridge to prevent troops crossing the canal. The group, which included Liam Ó Briain, spent Monday night occupying this row of houses.

De Coeur ordered that they request the occupants to 'Open in the name of the Republic', lest they be classed as 'mere burglars'. In one house, Ó Briain had the 'heart-breaking' task of barricading the doors with the owner's 'beautiful, costly furniture' and felt compelled to leave a note of apology behind. On Tuesday morning, a message delivered from Mallin by Margaret Skinnider called half the party back, and later the rest were ordered to follow.[37] They had not been under any great pressure and the reasoning behind this decision is unclear.

As the main body of Mallin's force bedded down on Monday night in Stephen's Green – many of them in the open despite the fact that the week's brilliant sunshine had been briefly replaced with wind and rain – British machine gunners silently made their way from Dublin Castle, past Trinity College and up Kildare Street before occupying the Shelbourne Hotel and United Services Club. Although barely thirty yards away they were able to avoid detection by the rebels. In the Shelbourne Hotel the troops posted guards at the doors, snipers at the windows and brought machine guns to the windows of the fourth floor. At 4.00am on Tuesday morning, the forces in the Shelbourne Hotel and the United Services Club, supported by troops on Merrion Row, opened fire across the Green. The men in the trenches tried to move to shelter in the shrubbery while women stationed in the park's summerhouse hid behind an embankment.[38]

James O'Shea was in his trench facing Dawson Street when:

> All the bushes and the trees got it. I had to lie down for
> nearly half an hour. …When the machine-gun fire stopped,
> snipers opened on any known trenches and I got hell for
> about an hour or more.'

O'Shea heard a scream, telling him that someone had been hit.[39]

Most of Mallin's force were on the Shelbourne (northern) side of the Green and were forced to retreat under heavy fire away from the railings on that side. O'Shea dodged from tree to tree, bullets hitting the trees assuring him 'that the men on the other side knew their business'. While crossing a bridge in the park O'Shea was narrowly missed by a bullet that ricocheted off the stonework beside him.[40] Thomas O'Donoghue had been given charge of the area around the gate at the Shelbourne Hotel and had decided to strengthen the barricade at that end by running the chains from the gate through the vehicles that had been used to block the street. While he and two others were engaged in this task the machine-gun fire began. One of the men, concentrating intently on his work, was slow to retreat and wounded by the fire. O'Donoghue and another ICA man took refuge in a rifle pit, only to find that it was far from the correct size. O'Donoghue was in the process of admonishing his colleagues when machine-gun fire fell over their heads.

To protect themselves they were forced to hastily enlarge the trench using a penknife and bayonet. O'Donoghue then retreated to find Mallin and seek orders. He was told to return to his trench and 'sit tight'.[41] As the military fired down on the Green and Mallin's force returned the fire, W.G. Smith could hear 'the curious tap-tap of the machine gun, a sinister sound that one could never get wholly used to.'[42]

On Tuesday morning, soon after the machine-gun fire began, Mallin, realising he was now in a hopeless position, was forced to order a full retreat from the Green. Still under heavy fire, the garrison made their way towards the Cuffe Street gate and the College of Surgeons, women leaving first. Despite the intensity of the fighting around them, the evacuation seems to have been conducted in a remarkably calm manner. James O'Shea 'had to wait nearly an hour, as men were being moved in groups to the college and everything was being done in a very orderly fashion'.[43] When he was satisfied the Green was evacuated, Mallin told James O'Shea 'to get ready, it would be a terrible job to get to the College, as all fire was now concentrated on it.' The pair, followed by Mick Kelly, left the Green via the Cuffe Street gate and continued along York Street under the cover of the railings before crossing over to the College of Surgeons.[44] During the evacuation Mallin had a narrow escape; a bullet passed through his hat. He took off the hat and in a quiet tone remarked to Frank Robbins, 'Wasn't that a close shave,

Robbins?' Both Robbins and James O'Shea later heard that Mallin had dashed out in front of machine-gun fire to drag a wounded man to safety.[45] He may, in fact, have had two such escapes – Margaret Skinnider recalls standing next to Mallin when a bullet entered his hat. Again, he calmly took the hat off, looked at the hole and placed the hat back on his head.[46]

During Tuesday morning's evacuation of Stephen's Green, the garrison were given a taste of the feelings of the local 'separation women'. Their abuse, which had begun the previous day, had clearly brought the restraint of some of the men to breaking point. As Mallin neared the college, one of the women rushed forward 'with the intention of tearing at him.' James O'Shea was on the verge of bayoneting the woman when Mallin simply pushed the rifle aside and continued to make for the door.[47] Earlier, Frank Robbins had been attacked by a crowd armed with iron bars and a hatchet, and was about to fire at a female ringleader when Richard McCormick intervened.[48] Not all bystanders were hostile to the rebels, however. While riding her bicycle to the College of Surgeons to deliver a dispatch, Margaret Skinnider was quietly informed by two men who stepped onto the road in front of her that the path ahead was clear. Later, a woman shouted from a window to inform Skinnider that she was 'losing her gun' as it began to break through the pocket of her coat.[49]

The garrison suffered a number of casualties before and

during the evacuation of the Green. A teenager, James Fox, was killed inside the Green. The officer commanding the Shelbourne recorded that eleven rebels were killed before the evacuation of the Green, although James Stephens only notes seeing four bodies inside the railings while Frank Robbins believes only a small number were killed or wounded.[50] Some of the dead in Stephen's Green were buried in shallow graves; W.G. Smith saw a pair of boots sticking out through the soil.[51] James Stephens recalled seeing the body of a dying rebel lying inside the railings as the rain poured down upon him; 'His companions could not draw him in for the spot was covered by the snipers from the Shelbourne.'[52]

It is not known if the College of Surgeons was part of the original occupation plan. Mallin may have known about the arms stored in the building prior to the Rising and been instructed to search for them, or learned about them on Monday and made a decision to occupy the building then. Although the College of Surgeons was built solidly and served as a safe outpost, it was 'cold and uncongenial', made up of draughty rooms filled with body parts, specimens preserved in liquid and there was a strong reek of formaldehyde.[53] To secure the building, sentries were placed on each doorway and passwords applied,[54] while windows were barricaded with desks, benches and books. A number of rooms in the college were adapted to suit the needs of the insurgents. A ground-floor lecture room became a dining room and dormitory; a small section of the caretaker's quarters was used for cooking; the sick bay (another lecture hall) was off bounds to all but the wounded and first aid assistants; a mortuary was created in the examination theatre and anatomy room which included slabs for the dead, a cross and rough altar. Mallin's headquarters were on the first floor.[55]

With the occupation of the college complete, a number of riflemen were ordered by Mallin to occupy the roof. From there James O'Shea describes how:

> we were getting it hot and heavy. You could not stand up under any circumstances. Bullets and chips of stonework were flying in all directions. I remember thinking that there were good marksmen fighting us.'

ICA man Mick Doherty, seemingly oblivious to what was happening around him, was calmly eating a sandwich when he was struck and killed by machine-gun bullets – 'the side of his face seemed to be gone.[56]

On Tuesday, looting had became widespread in the centre of the city as civilians took advantage of the chaotic events. Brigadier-General W.M.H. Lowe arrived in Dublin that morning and assumed control of the British forces in the city. Martial law was proclaimed throughout the city and county. That afternoon the men who had been on the roof of the College of Surgeons came down and were given tea and cocoa and allowed some rest. While they were asleep, others constructed 'a kind of stage which was reached by means of a ladder, where a view could be made of the snipers.' William Partridge was badly injured when a trapdoor to the roof of the college fell on him. There was an accidental casualty when a rifle went off and the ricochet caught one of the men in the eye.[57] Liam Ó Briain, who had made his way from his outpost at Leeson Street bridge to the College of Surgeons soon after the evacuation of Stephen's Green, spent Tuesday night with four others on guard duty in one of the college's large rooms. Ó Briain's companions had fallen asleep and he himself struggled to stay awake when Mallin, 'hatless, otherwise as neat and dapper as he had been the previous day', burst into the room with his revolver. Mallin 'stood in front of the glassless window, took aim and fired. An answering shot seemed to whisk by his head. He took aim deliberately again and fired. "Got him," he said.' He had hit a sniper at the railings opposite.[58]

The garrison in the College of Surgeons had been subject to continuous machine-gun fire from a number of British posts. They were able to leave the building via a number of adjacent buildings and move back and forth from Stephen's Green via a barricade at a point that offered sufficient tree cover from the machine guns in the Shelbourne Hotel. On Tuesday evening, Mallin decided to counter-attack a number of the British posts in an effort to relieve the pressure on the garrison. He ordered a section of men to enter the Turkish

Baths (on Lincoln Place, opposite the College of Surgeons) and break through the houses towards South King Street and then Grafton Street. James O'Shea recalls having to cross a narrow wooden plank, thirty feet up, from the roof of the college to the baths. As well as his ammunition, O'Shea carried a 7lb sledgehammer. The men broke through the walls using sledgehammers before searching each premises for occupants and useful rations, and barricading doors and windows.[59] This operation was carried out firstly to allow rebel occupations of these buildings but also with the ultimate aim of putting out the machine gun in the United Services Club and setting fire to other British-occupied buildings in the area, the latter aim ending in failure.[60] Those who had been sent out on such tunnelling missions spent much of the rest of the week engaged in smashing through walls and making sporadic return trips to the College of Surgeons.

On Wednesday afternoon a small band of insurgents fighting in No. 25 Northumberland Road and Clanwilliam House inflicted over two hundred casualties on British forces. However, Wednesday also brought the first signs that the tide was turning against the rebels, though Mallin's garrison were probably unaware of developments. At 8.00am the gunboat *Helga*, which had sailed up the river Liffey, began shelling the empty Liberty Hall. Seán Heuston's small force in the Mendicity Institute had been under heavy fire for two days and was completely outnumbered. At midday he surrendered. Meanwhile, the work of tunnelling to Grafton Street continued. A number of men, including Robbins and O'Shea, broke into the Alexandra Ladies' Club. The ladies did their best to be allowed to stay, but were forced to leave – clearly upset at the occupation of their club, they seem to have gone immediately to the military. Shortly after they had left, a telephone in the building rang. Unwisely, Captain O'Neill decided to answer. The telephone was directly in front of a window and almost at once a burst of machine-gun fire came through the window, narrowly missing its target. Unharmed and having laid flat for a period, the men continued to move through the buildings, leaving two or three behind to guard the ladies' club.[61]

A section of men under Robert de Coeur (of which Liam Ó Briain was a member) were ordered on Wednesday to occupy an island of houses between York Street corner and Proud's Lane, also breaking through from house to house and barricading doors and windows as they went. Unlike the rest of Mallin's garrison, de Couer's section appears to have been quite inactive on Wednesday in terms of fighting. They had instead, for example, spent a considerable amount of energy sawing through a set of stairs in a clever attempt to injure any attacking soldiers who felt they had just found an easy position to occupy. The attack never came. Where the men in the building in Stephen's Green north had been continuously firing at snipers, de Couer's group, mostly armed with shotguns, had not fired a shot at the enemy. They had been relieved to be assigned to occupy the houses in the first instance as it had given them something to do.[62] Jacob's biscuit factory was only a short distance from the area in which de Couer was based and the men there also had very little fighting to do during the week.

On Wednesday night Mallin somewhat reluctantly agreed to a proposal by Joe Connolly and Margaret Skinnider to lob some of the homemade (and not necessarily reliable) Liberty Hall bombs through the front windows of the Shelbourne Hotel. Prior to the planned bombing, a group of men under Thomas O'Donoghue were sent by Mallin to pressurise British troops at the Russell Hotel on Harcourt Street and if unable to hold their position to hamper the troops' retreat by burning some of the surrounding buildings. Skinnider was asked to lead a group of four to burn an antique shop in Harcourt Street. With Skinnider were William Partridge and Fred Ryan, one of the keen teenagers who had joined the garrison on Monday. As Partridge smashed the windows of the building they were to burn, Skinnider received a number of bullet wounds. Fred Ryan was shot dead. Partridge and another member of the group managed to carry their injured colleague back to the College of Surgeons. Though very badly wounded, she survived and later wrote that when Mallin saw her he said he 'could not forgive himself as long as he lived for having let me go on that errand.' Skinnider tried to cheer Mallin up by informing him that the plan to bomb the Shelbourne (which was then cancelled) would have been much more dangerous.[63]

On Thursday, fighting intensified in many areas of the city as the British began an assault on some of the rebel garrisons. Fierce house-to-house fighting took place in the Four Courts area, while an attack was launched on Éamonn Ceannt's position in the South Dublin Union, resulting in a stalemate. James Connolly was seriously injured in the ankle as he gave instructions on Middle Abbey Street.

A military cordon had effectively separated the garrisons to the north and south of the river and communication had ceased between the College of Surgeons and the rebel head-quarters in the GPO as the delivery of dispatches became impossible, further isolating the garrison there. Chris Caffrey, a member of Cumann na mBan, had acted as a message car-rier while disguised as a war widow, but was intercepted by British troops while carrying a dispatch from Mallin to the GPO. Caffrey was forced to eat the dispatch. When a soldier noticed her chewing something, Caffrey casually offered him a sweet from a bag she had in her pocket. She was released shortly afterwards.[64] Robert de Couer's section, who had not yet seen any fighting, were asked to provide covering fire to a group led by a rebel who had cycled to Merrion Street 'look-ing for a fight' and were retreating via their post. The firing alerted the British, previously unaware of their presence, to the rebels' position and the British turned their machine guns towards them. When the firing subsided, Liam Ó Briain was ordered to procure a nightdress for the wounded Margaret Skinnider and report back to the College of Surgeons. On his return, Ó Briain noted 'a more serious and grim air' than Wednesday. The siege-like conditions, constant barrages from British posts and the growing expectation of a large scale assault on the building was clearly beginning to take its toll on the men and women in the college. Markievicz, however, remained as keen to fight as ever, as Liam Ó Briain noted during a short conversation the same day: '[Markievicz] said she wanted to have a bayonet or something, "some stabbing instrument" for action at close quarters. "You are very blood-thirsty," smiled Mallin.'[65]

The number of wounded must have had a profound effect. Frank Robbins and three others, of similar height, had the difficult task of transporting Margaret Skinnider from one bed to another without a great loss of blood. According to Robbins:

> With plenty of time on our hands during Thursday, we moved around the different posts inside the College. Although there was intense fighting going on all the time, we were relatively safe in the College. We now had time to speculate on what was going on elsewhere in Dublin, but our only contact with the other units engaged in the Insurrection was through the dispatch carriers. We were

not, however, appraised of the information contained in these dispatches.[66]

On Thursday night Robbins was sent back to the post he had occupied on Wednesday after a meal and a final briefing.

Hunger, fatigue and the often siege-like conditions combined to create an almost surreal experience for the garrison during the first four days of the rebellion. This was further enhanced by a number of unusual incidents. One of the oddest involved the ducks in Stephen's Green: the park keeper, Jim Kearney, lived in a cottage in a corner of the park and twice a day a ceasefire was observed by the British forces and the garrison in the College of Surgeons to allow Kearney to feed the ducks.[67] Then, in one of the outposts on Wednesday, Mick Kelly shot a sniper dressed as a woman.[68] The conditions of insurrection even failed to stifle male desires: a young ICA man regularly deserted his post on York Street to secure hair oil and slip over to the College of Surgeons to visit one of the girls there. He was given a mock court martial and reminded of the penalty for deserting a post.[69]

One of the key problems facing Mallin's garrison throughout Easter Week was a lack of food and other supplies, and this is one aspect of the Rising that is often apparent in the memoirs of members of the garrison. Unlike those stationed in the nearby Jacob's biscuit factory, who were able to gorge on biscuits and cakes (though this brought its own problems as the week continued), there was no obvious source of food in the Green. There seems to have been little done to address this issue on Easter Monday. Towards the end of the week a hungry Liam Ó Briain was wondering, 'why hadn't we raided the Russell and Shelbourne hotels first thing on the Monday?'[70] Harry Nicholls had his first meal on Tuesday morning.[71] The move to the College of Surgeons did little to remedy the shortage of food. While the college was a sturdy and well-built post and offered protection from British machine guns, there was little in the way of edible goods (just two eggs and some tea) in the building. After a dispatch from Chris Caffrey – delivered in her British army widow's disguise – to Jacob's, MacDonagh informed William Oman, an ICA member who spent some of the fight with MacDonagh's garrison, that the College of Surgeons 'was in a really bad way for food'. MacDonagh sent a group of men (including several from the Citizen Army), carrying sacks of cakes and flour, to reinforce Mallin's garrison.[72] It often fell to the women to secure food for the garrison. Chris Caffrey and others spent the week either buying or taking goods from shops in the area. Mary McLaughlin, a fifteen-year-old member of Clann na Gael (a version of Na Fianna for girls), was in Stephen's Green on Monday, but moved to the GPO. There, James Connolly enquired about the condition of the men in the Green. When McLaughlin reported a shortage of food, Connolly gave a sum of money[73] with

which to buy whatever food she could. Unable to buy anything, McLaughlin made her way to the College of Surgeons
and offered Mallin the money. Mallin 'said it was no use to
him, what he wanted was food and ammunition.' She again
reported to Connolly. Her account described the situation
as follows:

> I ... gave back the money ... saying the men wanted food
> and ammunition. The two other women – Julia Grennan
> and Elizabeth Farrell – and myself volunteered to bring
> some ammunition to the College of Surgeons. ... I delivered
> the ammunition. But they still asked for food. I returned to
> the G.P.O. and reported the want for food. Mrs. Skeffington
> volunteered to carry the food with me if I would show her
> the way. She carried a big sack of food from the G.P.O.[74]

Nellie Gifford managed to secure some oatmeal and 'made
pot after pot of the most delicious porridge'. Still, Markievicz recorded that on Tuesday and Wednesday 'we absolutely
starved.'[75] The lack of provisions was felt even more keenly
in the outposts. Liam Ó Briain was given a loaf of homemade bread on Easter Monday which he ate on Tuesday in
the College of Surgeons. On Wednesday he had been sent
to occupy buildings around Leeson Place. Numerous trips
to the College of Surgeons to secure rations for the fourteen men at his outpost proved unsuccessful ('our little outpost was out of sight and out of mind'). Finally, on Friday

Ó Briain was able to secure some boiled rice from Nellie Donnelly. This was the only food they had eaten since Tuesday. On Saturday a supply of food was sent out to them from Jacob's and some bacon sent from the College of Surgeons. The men decided to postpone eating the bacon and to have a 'Sunday dinner' next day.[76] The men who had been tunnelling towards Grafton Street were brought some supplies by Nellie Gifford, and Gifford was able to return to the College of Surgeons with a large supply of brandy, whiskey and wine found in an occupied building. 'We had many problems to discuss that night,' Frank Robbins remembered of Thursday, 'but I think foremost in our thoughts was the question of obtaining food.'[77] The food problem, one that had become a serious issue by Friday, was quite spectacularly resolved by Saturday as Robbins and a number of others managed to tunnel into a pastry shop they had been searching for since Thursday. The men were further buoyed by the news of supplies sent from Jacob's.[78] Solving the food crisis seemed to provide a much needed, but ultimately short-lived, boost to Mallin's force.

A noticeable feature of Mallin's Rising was his ability to maintain a high level of discipline among his garrison, despite the conditions they faced. William Oman, a Citizen Army member who had been with Thomas MacDonagh in Jacob's factory before joining the garrison in the Royal College of Surgeons, immediately noticed the disciplined regime under

Mallin: 'I found things very different in the College of Surgeons to what they were in Jacob's. Commandant Mallin had a very, very strict code of discipline prevailing in the building.' He also noted that 'Due to the fact that there were so many injured in the College… no noise or hilarity was allowed … whereas in other posts there would have been singing and laughing.'[79] In a diary written in Kilmainham Gaol after the Rising, Madeleine ffrench-Mullen wrote 'he [Mallin] kept strict discipline … from the Countess [Markievicz] down without any exception of persons or place an order was an order and had to be obeyed instantly and to the letter.' Frank Robbins, a teetotaller, was threatened with court martial by ffrench-Mullen for refusing to obey a senior officer when he refused to take spirits she had offered as medicine.[80] Thomas O'Donoghue found a set of bagpipes in the College of Surgeons on Thursday morning which he decided to bring outside 'for a little recreation with them.' Having played them for about five minutes, O'Donoghue recalls that a message was sent to him to stop as it was believed that the wounded Margaret Skinnider was dying, 'and so my piping career was cut short'.[81] Shortly after the surrender, Diarmuid Coffey met Laurence Kettle, who had been kept as a prisoner by Mallin's garrison. Kettle told Coffey that 'there were a lot of boys from the roughest parts of the city but that they even took the trouble not to drop cigarette ashes on the carpets! … the boys there had time to escape after the surrender but said they were men of honour and would stick to their surrender.' Coffey was also informed that the College of Surgeons was 'in an awful mess but there was no wanton damage done there.'[82] During the fighting some younger members of the garrison had slashed an oil painting of Queen Victoria that had been hanging in the college. Mallin severely reprimanded those responsible and threatened to shoot anyone who carried out any similar acts of vandalism.[83] The garrison in the College of Surgeons had to make and fold their beds and those available had to assemble for the rosary, said by William Partridge, at a given time each day. Catholicism was a dominant feature of life in the College of Surgeons, so much so that Markievicz later claimed that it was the faith shown by Mallin and Partridge that prompted her own decision to convert to the Catholic faith.[84] On an excursion to the College of Surgeons from his outpost, Liam Ó Briain was annoyed at the length of time he was forced to wait to gain entrance. To Ó Briain's rough language, one of the men who answered the door responded: 'Give over that bad talk ... and we all after being to the priest and trying to keep good.' Ó Briain felt aggrieved that the privilege of having a priest did not extend to the garrison's outposts.[85] That Mallin was able to create such a controlled and disciplined environment and demand so much under strained circumstances is commendable. Mallin may have made military mistakes, but during the Rising he clearly earned the respect and admiration of those he commanded. This was picked up by R.M. Fox, who said of Mallin: 'he endeared himself to his men by his general attitude of consideration for them and the comradeship he had for everyone in the ranks. He was that rare combination – a good soldier who had not allowed any of his human feelings to be blunted.'[86]

During the Rising, the role of women was largely one of 'peripheral tasking'. Éamon de Valera excluded women entirely from his garrison, and while he was the only commandant to do so, the leaders of the other rebel posts had not made much provision for women either. Many women spent the Rising as nurses or cooks. Even these roles were often last-minute arrangements designed to keep the men free for combat.[87] In Stephen's Green, Madeleine ffrench-Mullen was in charge of the medical station and she continued this role in the College of Surgeons. Nellie Gifford was tasked with cooking what little food was available. The shortage of food was a serious issue in the College of Surgeons and it was the women who were assigned to purchase or commandeer supplies from surrounding buildings. Of the few women who did take a military role, most were members of the ICA garrisons. Mallin appointed Constance Markievicz as his second-in-command (however, this too was a last-minute improvisation). Margaret Skinnider was wounded attacking the Russell Hotel. Other women, such as Chris Caffrey, took on the potentially dangerous task of delivering messages to rebel headquarters and Mallin's outposts. Despite the increased military role of a small number of the women in Mallin's force, others were extremely disappointed with the role they were allotted. Marie Perolz was initially immensely proud at having been asked to operate as a messenger – 'Said Mallin with his heavenly smile "Is it dangerous enough for you?"' – but this pride was soon replaced with a 'bitter feeling of frustration' at not having been involved in the fighting.[88] While women were placed in harm's way to a greater extent in Mallin's than in other garrisons there is still evidence that this was done with some reluctance. Had there been greater numbers available it is unlikely that women would have taken such an active role – Mallin's reaction to the news that Skinnider had been wounded testifies to this.

Despite the intense firing that continued right through Friday, those who participated in the fighting in the College of Surgeons and its outposts recall little of note. By this stage the vivid descriptions that often characterise the statements of those who fought in 1916 are notable by their absence. Fatigue and the constant stress and pressures of the environment brought about a change in atmosphere. Douglas Hyde, who spent the Rising in the city, noted that by Friday the College of Surgeons had become 'the principal storm centre in this part of the city'. By Friday the surrounding streets were practically deserted and this 'heightened the all-pervasive sense of claustrophobia inside the college.'[89] The growing British domination of the city, in particular the area around the GPO, meant that Mallin's force became almost completely isolated from headquarters and the other rebel garrisons, resulting in a dearth of information regarding the situation in the rest of the city. Mallin and Markievicz offered insipid reassurances that all was going well, but in reality the garrison had no definite idea of what was happening around them. The emotional and physical strain brought about by fatigue, lack of food and the week's events was heightened by the expectation of a large-scale British assault that could come at any moment and wipe them out, as well as the continuing sounds of heavy fire and artillery on Friday. In preparation for this assault, the wounded were transferred from the College of Surgeons to a nearby hospital.[90] However, by Saturday afternoon the firing had died down considerably. Unknown to the garrison, an unconditional surrender had been agreed to by rebel headquarters. The GPO had been subject to an assault by British artillery and by Friday evening was on fire. The decision was taken to evacuate the building and occupy a row of buildings on Moore Street. On Saturday morning the leaders there voted almost unanimously to a surrender to prevent a further loss of life, with Thomas Clarke the only dissenter. Nurse Elizabeth O'Farrell, who had been treating wounded rebels in the GPO, delivered a message from Pearse to Brigadier-General Lowe, who had been in charge of operations in Dublin, to negotiate surrender. Pearse was informed that only an unconditional surrender would be accepted and at 3.45pm Patrick Pearse signed the order in front of General Sir John Maxwell, who had been appointed to oversee the suppression of the Rising and had arrived in Dublin in time to take the official surrender. The surrender order was co-signed by James Connolly to include the men under his own command in Moore Street and those in the Stephen's Green command.

Surrender

The order to surrender was delivered to each rebel garrison over the course of Saturday and Sunday. Nurse Elizabeth O'Farrell, who had been treating the wounded in the GPO, was assigned to deliver the orders. As one of the garrisons south of the river, the College of Surgeons did not receive the official surrender order on Saturday. Instead, they spent Saturday at the mercy of various rumours which were circulating. Nobody, however, expected the news that was to come. On Sunday word was sent out to all those posted outside the College of Surgeons to return for what many seem to have assumed was a short visit. Liam Ó Briain and his party left the bacon secured on Saturday behind them ('Nobody could imagine that we were going to abandon our precious bacon permanently').[91] Elizabeth O'Farrell had delivered Pearse's surrender order, co-signed by Connolly, to the College of Surgeons early that morning. Having seen

the order Mallin did not immediately respond, as evidenced
by the fact that O'Farrell was criticised by the British officer
in charge of taking Mallin's surrender, Major de Courcy
Wheeler, for not getting a definite answer.[92] Mallin seems to
have sent a dispatch to Thomas MacDonagh in Jacob's biscuit
factory, presumably to establish the legitimacy of the order
and what MacDonagh was planning to do, though without reply.[93] A 'council of officers' was called in the College
of Surgeons to discuss the order. Mallin announced that he
had received an order to surrender and that Connolly had
verified the order for all ICA men. While a small number
believed they should fight on, the majority decided that they
should obey the orders of their superiors. After this meeting
the garrison were assembled and Mallin read out the surrender order, apparently breaking down at least once before
regaining his composure. *Dublin's Fighting Story* records how
this process was repeated on three occasions as the men from
various outposts were summoned back to the College of Surgeons. While Mallin delivered the news, his friend William
Partridge 'stood by him with his arm around him'.[94] Thomas
O'Donoghue recollects that after the order was read:

> Captain Bob de Coeur and myself whispered together con-
> cerning the advisability of putting Mallin under arrest and
> continuing the fight, but Mallin, seeing us whispering and
> knowing both of us quite well, smiled and said: 'I know
> what you are talking about.'[95]

Frank Robbins had left the college on Saturday to secure a tweed suit (which was several sizes too large) and James O'Shea had been ordered to dump his uniform and obtain civilian clothes.[96] Both Robbins and O'Shea understood that they were obtaining civilian clothes to ease their escape to the mountains were they would continue a guerrilla fight. This seems to have been Mallin's plan too before he received the order to surrender. As will be seen later, he had actually discussed this with his wife before the Rising and must have told some of those under his command that they were to do this. Once he had verified that Connolly's order was legitimate, however, Mallin, like the other rebel leaders, was adamant that as they had fought as soldiers they must obey the orders of their superiors and surrender as soldiers.[97] James O'Shea recalls having a long argument with Mallin about the decision to surrender. As they argued, a sudden burst of machine-gun fire was heard and O'Shea pushed Mallin out of the way; Mallin said cryptically, 'Let it be now rather than later, as I and many of our friends will not live long.'[98]

Unsurprisingly, the reaction of the garrison to the surrender was a highly emotional one. Joe Connolly 'nearly went mad' noted James O'Shea. Robbins claimed that 'at that moment the act of surrender was to each one a greater calamity than death itself' while O'Donoghue retired to a separate room where he 'sobbed bitter sobs and cried bitter

Right: Markievicz (second from right) and Mallin (on her right) after the surrender of the Stephen's Green garrison. Both Markievicz and Mallin look remarkably relaxed.

Below: Interior of the College of Surgeons after the Rising. In his account of Easter Week, Diarmuid Coffey said that he had heard the college was 'in an awful mess but there was no wanton damage done there'.

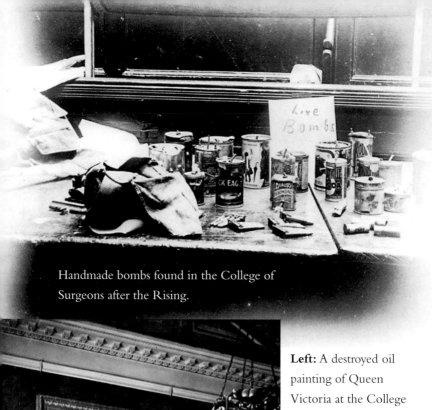

Handmade bombs found in the College of Surgeons after the Rising.

Left: A destroyed oil painting of Queen Victoria at the College of Surgeons. Mallin was furious with the young man who had slashed the painting, and he threatened to shoot anyone who carried out further acts of destruction of property.

Above: Cars at a barricade on Abbey Street. Similar barricades were constructed by Mallin's force around Stephen's Green.

Below: Post-Rising destruction at O'Connell bridge. The British army used artillery on the north side of the city. Mallin's position, however, was not bombarded.

Above: The Dublin Bread Company building on O'Connell Street was almost completely destroyed during the Rising due to the British bombardment of the GPO and any buildings that were in the vicinity.

Left: The GPO destroyed. The GPO served as headquarters for the forces of the Irish Republic during Easter Week.

Irish Rebellion - May 1916.
Soldiers bivouacking opposite Liberty Hall,
the Rebel Headquarters in Dublin.

Above: British soldiers opposite Liberty Hall after the suppression of the Rising. A flute believed to have been played by Mallin before the Rising was found in Liberty Hall when the building was searched by British soldiers.

Below: General Maxwell, who confirmed the death sentences of the executed leaders, reviewing Red Cross volunteers in the aftermath of the Rising.

The cells in Kilmainham Gaol that housed some of the rebel leaders before their execution. Mallin's wife and family visited him there on the eve of his execution.

Above: Mallin's second-in-command, Countess Markievicz, on her return to Dublin following her release from prison in 1917.

Below: The Mallin family after the Rising. Left to right: Séamus, Joseph, Seán, Agnes, Una. Centre: new baby, Maura, born 103 days after her father's execution.

& said for me loved wife, my life is numbered by hours now darling. I am drawing nearer and nearer to god, to that good god who died for us, you and I love, and our children, and our childrens children, god and his Blessed mother again and again Bless and protect you Oh saviour of man if my dear ones could die and enter heaven with me how Bless and happy I would they would be away from the cares and trials of the world Una my little one be a Nun joseph my little man be a Priest. if you can james & john to you the care of your mother make yourselves good strong men for her sake and Remember Ireland good By my wife my darling. Remember me, god again Bless and Protect you and our children I must now Prepare these last few hours must be spent with god alone

Your loving Husband Michael Mallin
Commandant
Stephens Green Comman

I enclose the Buttons off my sleeve keep them in memory of me
Mike xxxxx

Michael Mallin's last letter to his wife, Agnes.

tears… I found I was not alone in my grief. I saw men in all postures overcome by grief.'[99]

The surrender of the Stephen's Green garrison was due to be taken at midday and the garrison were ordered to dump all arms and assemble. Mallin told them that if anyone wanted to escape they could do so and no less would be thought of them. It seems this offer was not widely accepted. Harry Nicholls recalls that before they marched out to surrender officially, 'Commandant Mallin came along and ordered all officers to get back to the ranks saying that the British knew himself and Countess Markievicz, but there was no use in any of the others, as he put it, sacrificing themselves.'[100] Thomas O'Donoghue asked Mallin if he could take a set of bag-pipes to play as they marched, but was told that to take them would be 'tantamount to looting'.[101] The tricolour that had been flying at the College of Surgeons since Monday was lowered and in its place a white flag raised. Major de Courcy Wheeler took the surrender of the Stephen's Green garrison, including 109 men and ten women, from Michael Mallin and Countess Markievicz. Mallin presented Wheeler with a walking stick as a memento and Markievicz, in a typically theatrical gesture, kissed her gun before handing it over.[102]

The College of Surgeons garrison was marched by Brit-ish soldiers to Dublin Castle and soon after proceded via the Ship Street gate to Richmond Barracks in Inchicore. As was the case with many of the surrendered garrisons, those from the College of Surgeons were treated with hostility and distain by the general public. When they had made it as far as Grafton Street, William Oman claims that a 'mob attempted to attack us.' Only the action of the British officer who threatened to shoot those who refused to step back prevented an ugly scene.[103] On Dame Street, the group were jeered by members of the Dublin Fusiliers who had fought with the British army in the Great War. Markievicz was picked out for individual mocking. In the yard of Dublin Castle they passed a large pit: 'We were told [by the soldiers] that in an hour's time we would be in it', recalled Ó Briain. Later, on Thomas Street, they were subjected to aggressive shouts of 'Bayonet them' from the 'separation women' of the area. Despite the negative reaction from most people, Liam Ó Briain has stated that a soldier marching past remarked, in a thick Dublin accent: 'Why in the name – didn't yiz wait till the war'd be over? We'd ha' been with yiz. I fired over your heads the whole week.'[104] Markievicz later said that as they walked she had a rather morbid discussion with Mallin about whether they would be shot or hanged.[105] The garrison eventually arrived in Richmond barracks in Inchicore. After a period in the barrack's gymnasium, Mallin was separated from the rank and file, and marked for court martial.

Chapter 9

1916
Court Martial; Execution;
Last Words

In total, 187 civilians were tried by military court after the Rising; of that total, twenty-two were tried by general court martial and 165 by field general court martial. Easier to convene than a general court martial, a field general court martial required three officers, none of whom had to be legally trained and only the most senior had to hold a rank of captain or higher. For a death sentence to be passed, a unanimous verdict had to be reached. The sentence then had to be confirmed by the Commander-in-Chief, General Maxwell. The trials began on 2 May and most took place in Richmond barracks. Present at each trial were witnesses, detectives, three court martial officers and a prosecutor. It was decided by General Maxwell that the courts martial would be held *in camera* (not open to the public) and the official records of the trials were not opened to the public until 1999. Generally, during field general courts martial the 'right of the accused ... to call witnesses and cross-examine those who were called for the prosecution was at the discretion of the court, but was rarely, if ever, denied', according to historian Brian Barton. For the accused to have legal representation was extremely rare and lawyers were not allowed. Eleven of the 187 who were court-martialled after the Rising were aquitted, while a sentence of death was passed on eighty-eight. Fifteen sentences were confirmed by Maxwell and executions carried out.[1]

Michael Mallin's field general court martial took place in Richmond barracks on 5 May 1916; he was prisoner number seventy-eight. During the court martial two charges were put before Mallin. The first was the charge put before all those tried by court martial:

> Did an act to wit did take part in an armed rebellion and in the waging of war against His Majesty the King, such act being o [sic] such a nature as to be prejudicial to the Defence to [sic] the realm and being done with the intention and for the purpose of assisting the enemy.[2]

The second charge was that Mallin 'Did attempt to cause disaffection among the civil population of His Majesty.' Mallin pleaded not guilty to both charges. He was found guilty of the first charge and sentenced to death, but not guilty of the second, lesser charge.[3] Of the leaders executed for their role in the Rising, only Mallin, James Connolly (tried 9 May) and Seán MacDiarmada (tried 9 May) were accused of the second charge of causing 'disaffection'. There is no clear reasoning behind this, as Countess Markievicz, tried on 4 May, also faced both charges.

Mallin's court martial was presided over by Brigadier E.W.S.K. Maconchy; William G. Wylie served as prosecutor. Maconchy had, like Mallin, served in the Tirah campaign in India. Three prosecution witnesses were called, two constables of the Dublin Metropolitan Police, John O'Connell and C. Butler, and Captain H.E. de Courcy Wheeler, who had taken Mallin's surrender at the Royal College of Surgeons. Mallin cross-examined both constables, but not de Courcy Wheeler. Captain Wheeler later noted that during the trial Mallin stated: 'I would wish it placed on record how grateful myself and my comrades are for the kindness and consideration which Captain Wheeler has shown to us during this time.'[4] This is not contained in the official court-martial records.

Mallin called one witness in his defence, Laurence Kettle, who had been held prisoner by the Stephen's Green garrison during Easter Week. Constable O'Connell was called by the prosecution to provide evidence of Mallin's nationalist involvement prior to Easter Week. He stated that Mallin was named as Chief-of-Staff of the ICA in the *Workers' Republic*. O'Connell also claimed that he knew Mallin for 'about 9 or 10 months' and 'I have seen him marching with the Citizen Army and he has marched with James Connolly and Countess Markievicz and he has led them in company with James Connolly.' Mallin's defence can only be seen as a concerted attempt to avoid a guilty verdict and he was clearly keen to convince the jury that he was part of the rank and file as, under cross-examination, O'Connell replied that he was unsure whether Mallin or Connolly was in command during marching and that he had only seen Mallin named as Chief-of-Staff in the *Workers' Republic*. The second state witness, Constable Butler, also testified that he had seen Mallin marching with the ICA and that he had seen Mallin outside Liberty Hall on Easter Monday 'generally organising the Citizen Army'. In response to cross-examination he answered that 'He [Mallin] has been on friendly terms with the police and I know nothing against his character.' In his evidence, Captain Wheeler described how Mallin and Countess Markievicz had surrendered to him at the Royal College of Surgeons along with 109 men and ten women.[5]

Mallin then made a statement in his own defence. He began:

> I am a silk weaver by trade and have been employed by the
> Transport Union as band instructor. During my instruction
> of these bands they became part of the Citizen Army and
> from this I was asked to become a drill instructor. I had

no commission whatever in the Citizen Army. I was never taken into the confidence of James Connolly.

Mallin also claimed that he was unaware of plans for the Rising and believed the men were going out for manoeuvres. When he arrived at Stephen's Green, as ordered by Connolly, 'the firing started and the Countess of Markievicz ordered me to take command of the men … I felt I could not leave them and from that time I joined the rebellion.'[6] Mallin was indeed a silk weaver by trade and had been a band instructor for the Irish Transport and General Workers' Union, but the rest is fabrication and a clear attempt to downplay his role in the planning and implementation of the insurrection, again with a view to being classed among the 'rank and file' and reduce the chance of a death sentence. By claiming it was Markievicz who had promoted him, rather than the inverse, Mallin, in Brian Barton's words 'threatened literally to place her in the firing line.' It was unsurprising that Mallin would want to avoid a death sentence and he probably believed that the British would not shoot Markievicz as she was a woman, but it remained 'a considerable risk to take with a loyal comrade's life, and hardly a chivalrous one.'[7] In her own trial, Markievicz pleaded not guilty to the main charge and guilty to the lesser charge of 'causing disaffection among the civilian population', but her sentence had not yet been confirmed and Mallin could not have known for certain that she was not to be executed when he made his statement.[8]

Mallin was keen to point out that he saved any civilians or prisoners in Stephen's Green and, inaccurately, that he 'gave explicit orders to the men to make no offensive movements and I prevented them attacking the Shelbourne Hotel.'[9] Mallin then called his defence witness, Laurence Kettle, who verified that 'The prisoner prevented my death by shooting. I was treated with every possible consideration and also I saw he [Mallin] did the same for any other prisoner.'[10] Mallin's desire to show the jury that prisoners were well treated was shared by some of the other leaders who were subsequently executed. Patrick Pearse asked the prosecution witness, Lieutenant King, 'Were you a prisoner in our hands and how were you treated?' Thomas Clarke also questioned King similarly.[11] In the case of Pearse and Clarke, their insistence on placing the treatment of prisoners on record is more indicative of concerns about the legacy of the Rising than any attempt to receive a favourable verdict.

Of the fourteen men who were tried in Dublin and executed in Kilmainham Gaol (Kent was tried in Cork and Casement in London), Mallin was one of the few to call a defence witness, further evidence of a concerted effort to avoid the firing squad. Patrick Pearse was not given the opportunity to call a witness. John MacBride called his landlady, Mrs Allen. Éamonn Ceannt was by far the most active in this regard and called three witnesses (he also called Thomas MacDonagh, but MacDonagh had already been executed). Con Colbert, conversely, was the only one of the fourteen not to cross-examine the prosecution witnesses; he also declined to make a statement in his defence.

Among the trial proceedings, Mallin's attempt to avoid a guilty sentence is the most striking. Mallin set out to give an untrue account of his actions in a definite attempt to mislead the jury. His attempt to place Markievicz as the leader of the garrison is particularly dishonourable. Comments made by Mallin after the surrender in the Royal College of Surgeons add a sense of futility to this attempt: upon being questioned as to the fate of the garrison, Mallin replied that he believed he would be shot.[12] William O'Brien also recalls that during a conversation in the gymnasium of Richmond barracks Mallin told him he expected to be shot.[13] As a former British soldier, it can also be imagined that Mallin was well aware of the court-martial process and the severity of the charges against him, perhaps helping to explain such a desperate defence. The evidence produced by the prosecution witnesses was, in many of the other cases, particularly thin and often inaccurate. The evidence given by the three prosecution witnesses in Mallin's case, however, was accurate and damning.

After the suppression of the Rising, General Sir John Maxwell was adamant that the leaders of the insurrection should be shot. Based on the criteria Maxwell was concerned with, namely previous nationalist activities, rank or role in the Rising and the number of British casualties inflicted in each area, Mallin was unlikely to escape a death sentence. In Maxwell's memorandum to the British Prime Minister Herbert Asquith, he noted of Mallin:

> He was in command of the rebels who occupied Stephen's Green and the College of Surgeons. At these places serious encounters took place and there were many casualties both amongst the military and civilians. He surrendered on 30 April and was accompanied by a body of 109 rebels all of whom were armed.[14]

Éamon de Valera was the only garrison commandant to escape execution and a number of those executed held lesser ranks than Mallin during the fighting, most notably William Pearse. It must also be noted that Markievicz, Mallin's second in command, seems only to have escaped the death penalty on the basis of her gender.

Mallin was transferred under escort to Kilmainham Gaol on the evening of his court martial, 5 May. On the way to the gaol Mallin passed his home in Inchicore. Looking out for a sign of his family, Mallin was only able to spot the family dog: 'the only one of my household that I could cast my longing eyes on was poor Prinie the *dog* she looked so faithful there at the door'.[15] Mallin, Con Colbert, Éamonn Ceannt, Seán Heuston and others attended mass on Sunday, 7 May.[16] Two other rebels who attended the mass met Mallin there. One, who recalls having a few words with Mallin, described it as 'an unforgettable scene'; another noted that of the group Mallin in particular looked 'very sad'.[17] Later that day Mallin was informed that General Maxwell had confirmed his death sentence.

Mallin's children spent the week of the Rising in the house of their mother's sister, Jane Thewlis, in Chapelizod. When the Rising had been suppressed, the eldest sons, James and Joseph, then aged twelve and ten respectively, along with their grandmother, Sarah Mallin, moved back into their grandparents' home in Kilmainham. Their mother and the younger children, Una and Joseph (aged eight and two), stayed with their uncle Thomas Mallin in Harold's Cross. Agnes had spent the week searching the city for news of her husband, but was unable to get any information. On the evening before Mallin's execution his family were informed that he wished to see them and a car was provided to convey them to Kilmainham Gaol. James and John were asleep when the car arrived to take them the short distance to the gaol. James remembers seeing an order on a piece of paper shown to his grandmother to which she replied, 'Mike's time is up.' His aunt Katie was unwilling to believe the news: 'But that can't be true.' The car carried James, John, Sarah and Bart Mallin, along with Katie, who 'sighed heavily'. This car may also have collected Mallin's wife, youngest children and brother Thomas, or they were conveyed in a separate car.

On his way to the gaol, Thomas Mallin ascertained from a member of the Dublin Metropolitan Police that his brother's sentence was, in fact, death.[18]

Michael Mallin was visited in his cell in Kilmainham Gaol by his wife Agnes, his sons James, John and Joseph, his daughter Una, his mother Sarah, his brothers Thomas and Bartholomew and his sister Katie. Mallin's father was at that time working as a carpenter for Jacob's biscuit company in a factory in Liverpool; he learned of his son's execution through reading a news report on the street.[19] The visit was a surreal experience for the children. There was a palpable sense from the adults that something terrible was happening, something they were unable to explain to the youngsters. Further, the late hour meant the children were not fully awake and Joseph seems to have slept through most of the visit. Mallin's eldest son, James (Séamus), has given his own memories of the visit:

> It was a big, darkish hall, with policemen and soldiers around us. People hardly spoke a word and when they did it was in a quiet, low voice. We were directed onwards past low doors on the left-hand side, each one similar to the other. I noticed a light, like the yellow light of a candle behind a door that was half-open and I heard mumbles as if the Rosary was being said. The next door was opened and we were let into a small room. My father was there standing before us, just as I always remembered him, a small

smile playing on his face but with no happiness in it; but with no bitterness either. He had a small blanket around his shoulders. I don't think he had a jacket on … I noticed a tall, dignified priest who had a long, black and white cassock on him. Years later I heard it was Fr Michael Browne OFM [Fr Browne seems to have entered the cell after the Mallin family had arrived]. There was another priest there as well I think but I didn't really see anyone except my father and my mother. 'I am to die tomorrow at dawn,' said my father. I'm not going to say anything about my mother's heartache. … My mother couldn't believe that this was the end. As for us, the children, we probably didn't really understand what was happening.

The reality of the situation was not easy to grasp for a twelve-year-old boy:

Before the Rising my father usually spoke to me as he spoke to grown-ups. Of course, I thought I was a grown-up already. But now, I was only a small child again with no understanding of the ways of the world, and with only one thought in my mind, that I wouldn't see my father again, something I couldn't believe.[20]

Michael Mallin spoke of Jimmy Fox, a teenager who had been killed under his command. He was the son of a widower and Mallin had known the family personally. He also mentioned William Partridge, who was 'like a beloved brother to me the whole time.' The first thing he said, however, was that he was to die at dawn. Agnes had never expected her husband to be executed. Mallin had apparently often discussed his plan to retreat to the mountains and mount a guerrilla campaign from there, and this is what she had expected to happen.[21] But instead, he had followed the surrender order of his superiors. The sentence of death came as an immense shock to her. Thomas Mallin has recalled how:

> After the surrender Agnes and I anxiously watched the papers for the results of the trials of the prisoners. We discussed what sentence he [Mallin] would get. Agnes spoke in terms of years, even twenty years. She never thought of a sentence of death.[22]

In Kilmainham Gaol, Thomas Mallin 'met the officer in charge of the guard who said to me, 'I will never forget what I saw in that cell, to hear an aged woman [Mallin's mother; she was only about sixty-two] say she was delighted to have her first son die for his country.'[23] When left alone with his brother, Thomas asked if the Rising and his execution had been 'worth it'. He has related Mallin's reply:

> It is worth it. Ireland is a grand country, but the people in it are rotters. The first Irishman to join the British army was a bastard. The British army is made up of them and gaolbirds and wasters. Some join through drink and some through lack of work. I will show my guards how an Irishman can

die for his own country – in his own country. I can die praying. If these men are sent to France they will die cursing. They will die on the ground, moaning, and not be able to see their mothers and their sweethearts.'[24]

If accurate, these comments are remarkable for a man who spent much of his life in the British army, although perhaps less surprising having come at what was a highly emotional time. It is not, however, the only example of Mallin's distaste for the British army. Liam Ó Briain has recorded that Mallin was 'proud' to say he had not been involved in the Boer War and has claimed that Mallin 'referred regularly to the DF's [Dublin Fusiliers] monument at the Grafton Street entrance to Stephen's Green as "traitors' arch".'[25] In his home in Inchicore there was a picture of the drums and flag of the Royal Scots Fusiliers that Mallin had made while in India ('We thought it was a lovely picture', said his son, 'not for what it showed but for how cleverly it was made'). In his cell, Mallin said this picture should be burned; he was immediately convinced otherwise by Fr Browne who pointed out, 'It would be better not to do that ... Better to have only charitable thoughts in your mind and in your heart when you go into the presence of our Lord.'[26]

The officer in charge was not alone in being profoundly affected by the intensely emotional scene in Mallin's cell. Fr (later Cardinal) Michael Browne was attending to Seán Heuston and felt 'as the weeping was intense' from Mallin's cell (which was nearby) that he might be needed there. He briefly left Heuston and on entering Mallin's cell remembered how 'my entrance causing surprise, the weeping momentarily ceased'. Mallin, 'serene though very much affected', then rose to greet Fr Browne who stayed with the family for some time before returning to Heuston.[27] Fr Michael Heuston, brother of Seán, was also in Heuston's cell when Mallin's family arrived: 'about 10.10, Fr Michael [Browne], hearing a commotion in the next cell and finding from the soldier that Mallin's wife had come to him, had gone in to see them. Jack [Seán Heuston] heard the crying, too, but said nothing.'[28]

Soon, Mallin's family left him for the last time. At the appointed time Father Augustine OFM, a Capuchin priest from Church Street in Dublin, accompanied Mallin to the firing squad in the stonebreakers' yard of Kilmainham Gaol. There he was executed between 3.45am and 4.00am on 8 May 1916. Éamonn Ceannt, Seán Heuston and Con Colbert were executed the same morning.

The *Catholic Bulletin* described Mallin's execution as follows: 'The story of his death is as fascinating as a romance, and as grand as an epic. He is said to have prayed into the very rifles of those who shot him, and his last aspiration was: "Lord Jesus, receive my spirit."'[29] Unsurprisingly, the *Catholic Bulletin* was keen to point to this as further evidence of Mallin's strong Catholic faith. The articles published at this time, emerging as they did so soon after the events of Easter Week, undoubtedly played a part in the popular perception of the Rising in the following years.

While the executions of the leaders of the 1916 Easter Rising were taking place, the Commander-in-Chief British troops in Ireland, General Sir John Maxwell, sent a memorandum to Prime Minister Asquith entitled 'Short History of rebels on whom it has been necessary to inflict the supreme penalty'. This memorandum gave a brief outline of each man's involvement in the nationalist movement and the Rising itself. The entry for Michael Mallin states:

> This man was second in command of the Larkinite or Citizen Army with which organisation he had been connected since its inception. He was in command of the rebels who occupied Stephens Green and the College of Surgeons. At these places serious encounters took place and there were many casualties both amongst the military and civilians. He surrendered on the 30th April and was accompanied by a body of 109 rebels all of whom were armed.'[30]

Last Words

On the evening before his execution Mallin wrote a last letter to his wife Agnes. This letter is the most striking piece to emerge from the writing of those awaiting the firing squad. The letter begins with a recognition of what is to come: 'My darling Wife Pulse of my heart, this is the end of all things earthly; sentense [sic] of Death has been passed, and a [sic] quarter to four tomorrow the sentense will be carried out by shooting'. There is an air of acceptance and resignation as Mallin continues, 'and so must Irishmen pay for trying to make Ireland a free nation.' An intense feeling of regret and sorrow then begins to spill from the writing:

> Oh my darling if only you and the little ones were coming too if we could all reach Heaven together my heart strings are torne to pieces when I think of you and them of our manly James, happy go lucky John shy warm Una <u>dadys</u> [sic] <u>Girl</u> and oh little Joseph my little man my little man Wife dear Wife I cannot keep the tears back when I think of him he will rest in my arms no more, to think that I have to leave you to battle through the world with them without my help.

Later, deeply affected by the fact that he would not see his children again, Mallin writes:

> a Father's Blessing on the heads of my children James John Una Joseph my little man, my little man, my little man, his name unnerves me again, all your dear faces arise before me God bless God bless you my darlings.[31]

The letter is deeply personal and is written as a near stream of consciousness, with little or no punctuation. It is an outpouring of emotion that had, perhaps, been kept in check until this point. In writing about those who will be left behind, the letter is tinged with regret, sorrow and distress. In relation to the cause, however, Mallin writes, 'I do not believe our Blood has been shed in vain. I believe Ireland will come out greater and grander.'[32] This is a common sentiment in the last written words of the other condemned leaders. Mallin's last letter has strong religious sentiments, unsurprising for a man about to die. Like many of the other condemned men, Mallin asks for his family and friends to pray for him. He also requests his wife to have a mass said. Towards the end of the letter, Mallin writes, 'Oh saviour of man if my dear ones could die and enter heaven with me, how Blessed and happy I would [be] they would be away from the cares and trials of the world'. Mallin requested his wife to see to it that his youngest son Joseph would become a priest and his daughter Una a nun 'so that we may have two to rest on as penance for our sins'.[33] This was a remarkable attempt to influence the lives of his children from beyond the grave. In their adult lives, Joseph Mallin joined the Jesuit order and Una Mallin became a Loreto nun. John Mallin also became a Jesuit priest. The letter finishes, 'God again Bless and Protect you and our children. I must now Prepare these last few hours must be spent with God alone.'[34]

Mallin made another remarkable request in his final letter, which was removed from the published version by Piarais

MacLochlainn, a member of the Kilmainham Gaol Restoration Committee, who edited a collection of the last writings of all the executed leaders:

> I would ask a special favour of you wife of my heart, but I leave you absolutely free in the matter dont [sic] give your love to any other man you are only a girl yet and perhaps it is selfish of me to ask it of you but my darling this past forghtnight [sic] has taught me that you are my only love my only hope.[35]

The letter is tinged with a strong sense, not only of the pain of separation from his family, but also of guilt at the position in which he would leave his family and, perhaps, his failings as a husband and breadwinner. It is this outpouring of guilt and worry that makes the letter such a remarkable piece of writing. '... we have now been married thirteen years ...', wrote Mallin, 'you have been a true loving wife too good for me, you love me my own darling think only of the happy times we spent together forgive and forget all else'. Another reference, also excluded by MacLochlainn, emphasises Mallin's guilt: 'I have sinned against you many times in the fulness of your pure holy love for me you will forgive me my many transgressions against you'.[36]

Mallin is acutely aware of the financial difficulties his young family will face and this troubles him greatly. He instructs his wife to visit Fr McCarthy who 'will see to the

Education and General welfare of our dear ones' (Fr McCarthy had just received Mallin's final confession), and Alderman Thomas Kelly as 'he ... will be able to help you for my sake as well as yours ... it is due to you as the Wife of one of the fallen'.[37] Even having written 'Pulse of my heart, good by [sic] for a while, I feel you will soon be in heaven with me', financial concerns again surface:

> if anyone comes to you for any money that I owe them investigate them and so far as lies in your power pay them. I am offering my life as atonement for all my sins and for any debts due but if any debt press undully on any one try and pay them for my sake.[38]

Mallin is torn between sorrow and guilt and these emotions flow from the page in turn. Attempts to justify the Rising or his decision to fight are dwarfed here by the human tragedy of what has happened.

Mallin's son has recalled that his father's greatest concern was the state his wife was left in as none of his children were old enough to earn a living.[39] A short letter, also written during Mallin's final hours, emphasises this concern – the original cannot be traced but it seems that the letter is authentic. The letter was written to Alderman Thomas Kelly and begins with a stark admission:

> I have left my wife and children absolutely destitute. Will you kindly look up Mr. R_____ [it is not clear who this

is] and the ladies of the Cumann nam Bam [sic]. They have, I believe, charge of things. I had nothing but my life to give to Ireland. That I freely give. You will, I know, accede to a request from a man who is to die at a quarter to four to-morrow morning. God bless you! God save Ireland!

This version of the letter was published in the *New York American* newspaper on 3 September 1916 under the heading 'Destitution Killing Irish'. The article was published to assist a fundraising drive in America for the dependants of those killed during the Rising. Mallin's letter was highlighted as one notable example of the poverty and want in Dublin following the rebellion. Alderman Kelly is mentioned in Mallin's letter to his wife so it is not unlikely that he would also have been written to. The clear punctuation and spelling does not fit with Mallin's letter-writing style and was probably edited for publication, but the reference to the shooting at 'a quarter to four to-morrow' and use of the phrase 'God bless you' certainly resonates with the letter to his wife.

Mallin wrote a third letter from his cell in Kilmainham Gaol – to his parents, John and Sarah. The original letter does not survive, although Piarais MacLochlainn published a corrected version of the letter based on a manuscript copy. MacLochlainn asserts that Mallin's son, John, confirmed the letter existed.[40] This letter, as published by MacLochlainn, seems to be a much more composed piece of writing. Mallin asks for forgiveness, writing, 'Forgive your poor son who is to meet his death ... Forgive him all his shortcomings towards you – this applies especially in the management of my father's business.'[41] This is possibly a reference to the family's boat-building business, although there is no evidence to indicate that Mallin was ever involved in the business. Mallin asks his family to pray for him before stating, 'I tried, with others, to make Ireland a free nation and failed. Others failed before us and paid the price and so must we.'[42] The end of the letter resonates with some passages from the letter to his wife:

> I have now but a few hours left. That I must spend in prayer to God, that good God who died that we might be saved. Give my love to all. Ask Uncle James [Dowling] to forgive me any pain I may have caused him. Ask Tom Price and all in the trade [silk weavers] to forgive me. I forgive all who may have done me harm.[43]

The letter to his parents is more comparable in style and tone to the letters of the other executed leaders. The raw emotion of Mallin's letter to his wife is missing but it is not unlikely that Mallin would have remained calm while writing to his parents and the letter does seem, for the most part, to be authentic.

In their profile of Michael Mallin for the 'Events of Easter Week' series, the *Catholic Bulletin* quoted selected segments of the letter to his wife, stating, 'his character is mirrored in the course of his last letter to his wife, written immediately before his execution.'[44] In a later article on the families of some of the deceased of the Easter Rising, the *Catholic Bulletin* again quoted from the letter, as 'this further extract from it will, we are sure, be eagerly welcomed.'[45] Much of the extract chosen emphasises Mallin's Catholicism. Also chosen were the most moving pieces of the letter; those relating to his young children. This letter would, to a large extent, have dictated the formation of the popular memory of Mallin that emerged in the early years after 1916.

The court-martial proceedings and final letters give an interesting insight into the character of Michael Mallin. During the surrender Mallin showed honour and bravery. He followed the orders of his superior and surrendered as a soldier should. He was willing, it seems, to forego some of this honour during his trial and lie in order to avoid a guilty verdict. It would appear from the letter to his wife that the guilt he felt at leaving her to raise their family alone was the foremost motivation for the manner in which he conducted his court-martial. In Mallin's letter to his wife there is not the calmness or serenity discernable in letters written by Pearse and others. As his court-martial proceedings would verify, Mallin does not appear to have been prepared to die so readily. Mallin looked on death as a punishment rather than a 'sacrifice' but some passages do disclose the defiance and pride about the motivation for the rebellion and the means through which it was carried out that is discernable in the last letters of other executed men. Mallin believed in the aims of the uprising and felt that sovereignty would be a step on the path to eradicating the social injustices that he had experienced and spent the latter half of his life fighting. In terms of the consequences of his execution, however, Mallin shows a far more developed sense of the loss and sadness that his imminent execution would cause for others, and significantly, for which he accepts full responsibility himself. Here is a portrait of a man who had two priorities in life, and for whom one tragically cost him the other.

• • • • •

Chapter 10

1916 – today
Critical Commentary on Mallin's Rising

Militarily, the events of Easter Week 1916 have drawn a significant amount of discussion and debate. The rebel leaders' performance; the plan for the Rising; the reaction of the British administration; the behaviour of the rebels and the behaviour of British forces are some of the key issues that have been scrutinised by historians. Michael Mallin's place in the literature of the 1916 Rising has been dictated by a number of key criticisms made by historians of some of the tactics he employed during the rebellion. While much of the criticism is valid, can an attempt be made to rationalise, at least in some way, some of the tactical decisions made during the week, including the decision to occupy Stephen's Green as a rebel base in the first instance?

How, for example, did contemporaries react to what they saw? What were the impressions of those who served under Mallin and how do they fit into what has been written about Mallin more recently? This chapter will attempt to analyse the recurring criticisms of Mallin's Rising and offer an assessment of his performance in light of the commentary of some of those who fought under his command.

There are several accounts from non-combatant witnesses to the action in Stephen's Green that add weight to the criticism that has dominated the discourse on Mallin and 1916. Douglas Hyde, founder of the Gaelic League and later first President of Ireland, accidentally stumbled across the opening moments of the Rising while on a trip for cigarettes. In his diary for 25 April he commented on the position of the rebels in Stephen's Green on Monday night. Hyde was certain that the Green would be evacuated by morning, noting that the trenches were too vulnerable to machine-gun and rifle fire from surrounding buildings.[1] Laurence Nugent spent Easter Week travelling around the city recording the fighting as he saw it. In his statement to the Bureau of Military History, based on the notes he made, Nugent pointed to some tactical failings of Mallin's garrison that he noticed:

> The Volunteers [sic] occupied a house at the junction of Lr. Leeson St and Adelaide Road but evacuated it on Tuesday. I wonder why as there was no threat of attack. They also

evacuated Davy's of Sth. Richmond Str. and Harcourt St station, but these two posts could be attacked from Portobello Barracks and there was only a few men to defend them. The early evacuation of Little's public house at the corner of Cuffe St seemed strange, as if it were attacked there was a good line of retreat to the College of Surgeons. The Citizen Army men who occupied these posts were by Wednesday confined to the College of Surgeons, and their scouting, if any, seemed defective.[2]

Liam Ó Briain, one of the men who had occupied the house at Leeson Street bridge, also claimed to have been unclear of the reasoning behind this evacuation.[3] It may have been the result of a shortage of numbers in the college, but the garrison there, although under continual fire, were reasonably secure. Furthermore, the same group were sent out of the college on Wednesday to occupy another set of buildings. On Wednesday, Nugent described how a British machine-gun corps (made up of 'territorials and poorly trained') had pushed fourteen machine guns from Kingstown (Dún Laoghaire) and halted on Leeson Street bridge. Nugent claimed:

I am well aware that the Volunteers in the College of Surgeons knew the position by the time the troops were on the move again, and had they sent out a dozen men they could have captured the machine-guns as these men were unable to fight. But nothing was done! The garrison in Jacob's or

Marrowbone Lane could also have captured them. I do not know if they knew of the presence of the guns.[4]

The tactical failings evident in these contemporary accounts have regularly resurfaced in the work of modern historians. Brian Barton and Michael Foy have claimed that during the Rising Mallin 'revealed himself as strategically unimaginative and organisationally deficient.'[5] The decision to occupy open ground in the first place has raised criticism. In 1968 F.X. Martin claimed that the occupation of Stephen's Green remained 'something of a mystery and an embarrassment'; later, Charles Townshend described the Green as 'a militarily hopeless position in the open'. Martin points to Connolly's approval of the site as evidence of 'wishful thinking' and as reason to question his ability as a strategist, while Townshend notes that responsibility for the decision itself is open to debate but 'the penalty for miscalculation was heavy and rapid.'[6]

In his *History of the Irish Citizen Army*, first published in the 1940s, R.M. Fox has claimed the plan for the Rising 'owed a great deal' to Connolly and Mallin. In Fox's eyes, the key reason behind the failure of the original plan was Eoin MacNeill's countermanding order that deprived the rebels of the numbers they had anticipated.[7] Fox claims that if the Rising had been carried out to the scale it was originally planned, the Stephen's Green garrison would have carried a far greater importance: 'It could have served as a central transport base, with lines of communication, capable of being used as a means of linking up rebel activities throughout the city, taking supplies, munitions or men wherever they were needed.'[8] Unfortunately, no detailed records survive outlining the plan for the Rising as envisaged by the military council and it is therefore impossible to assess the accuracy of Fox's remarks.

In 1967 Mrs Kathleen Clarke, wife of Tom Clarke (the first signatory of the Proclamation and one of the key movers behind the Rising), claimed that the Green was never intended for occupation by the military council, and that Mallin was immediately ordered to evacuate by dispatch from the GPO on Easter Monday. This would imply that either Mallin acted against orders (something which would appear to be very much out of character) or that the Green was occupied on the orders of James Connolly, without the approval of the rest of the military council. Neither of these explanations seems satisfactory and throws serious doubt on Mrs Clarke's claims. In reply, Frank Robbins pointed out that the Green was part of the plan outlined by Connolly to the members of the ICA, Robbins included, on the Tuesday before the Rising was due to begin.[9] James O'Shea claims that some time before the Rising, Mallin told him that he had been assigned to Jacob's factory and had even scouted the building from the roof and 'pointed out the possibilities for food and height that was contained in this huge building' as well as earmarking it as a location from which to command Dublin Castle and the Kevin Street Police Depot.[10] Later, O'Shea recalls spending an evening walking with Mallin around Stephen's Green 'taking notice of the high buildings – Shelbourne Hotel etc. – water in pond, entrance to Green from different angles.' During this walk O'Shea claims Mallin outlined the reasons for taking the Green:

> It was intended that at least 500 men would take over this area. It would be barricaded at different entrances, such as Merrion Street and the street at the Shelbourne Hotel and all streets leading to the Green. It was to be a base as it had all the necessities for a base. It had plenty of water; as he remarked water could be cut off in a long fight. It had hotels with plenty of food and beds. It also had a hospital – St Vincent's. It was intended also for prisoners.[11]

If O'Shea's account is accurate, then it would appear that Mallin was originally assigned to Jacob's biscuit factory but later reassigned to Stephen's Green.[12] Despite O'Shea's seemingly unrealistic estimate of five hundred men (the ICA numbered little over two hundred in 1916) his comments would suggest that Stephen's Green had been well assessed and, correctly or not, was seen as a suitable rebel stronghold. Moreover, as pointed out by Barton and Foy, the coordinated manner in which the Green was occupied on Easter Monday suggests careful planning and instruction rather than a hasty,

last-minute decision.[13] Kathleen Clarke's contention, therefore, that Mallin occupied the Green against the wishes of
the military council appears unlikely.

Stephen's Green does, however, remain something of an
anomaly when compared to the other sites taken by the
rebels. In every other garrison the rebels occupied large,
strategically located buildings and barricaded themselves
inside. As no official plan for the Rising has survived it is
impossible to say what the logic was behind the decision to
occupy Stephen's Green. That logic, whatever it may have
been, turned out to be utterly flawed. The layout of Stephen's Green, an open park surrounded by tall buildings
with little adequate shelter, demanded a different approach
and the approach taken by Mallin – the digging of trenches
– has been widely criticised. As with the choice of Stephen's
Green as a base, the responsibility for the idea is uncertain.
Again, it is unlikely that the decision was a last-minute one.
Mallin was likely either instructed to occupy the Green this
way or decided on the approach himself. From whomever
the idea came, it was doomed to failure. F.X. Martin wrote
that digging trenches rather than sending men to occupy the
Shelbourne Hotel, was the 'high point of futility.'[14] Similarly,
Townshend has noted, 'The reasoning behind this has never
been clear. Guests in the hotel … peered out in some baffle-
ment at the strange goings-on.'[15]

The excuse usually put forward by members of the garrison for the poor tactical deployment of men and the failure to occupy important strategic locations – the low turnout resultant from MacNeill's countermanding order – provides, in Fearghal McGarry's words, 'a convenient excuse rather than the reason for poor tactics'. According to McGarry the decision to deploy the men in trenches rather than the overlooking buildings 'made no sense regardless of numbers.'[16] Members of the garrison engaged in the actual digging do not seem to have questioned it, however. Liam Ó Briain recalls digging 'manfully until after six or seven o'clock'. Even Thomas O'Donoghue, who claimed to be a well read student of military tactics, recalled that one of his first tasks upon entering Stephen's Green was to mark where trenches were to be dug.[17]

Keith Jeffery has likened the scene in Stephen's Green to the landings in Suvla Bay in August 1915 when much of the 10th (Irish) Division of the British army was wiped out in a bloody battle with the Turkish army. As Jeffery points out, 'The decision to hold St Stephen's Green, and dig *trenches* there, without seizing all the buildings overlooking the park, closely matches, with less justification, the situation at Suvla where the Turks were able to fire down into the 10th (Irish) Division positions.[18]

Was the decision to dig trenches, then, simply an inexcusable, incomprehensible tactical disaster? There is a possibility that the idea of digging the trenches was, consciously or otherwise, influenced by events on the western front and, as seen previously, Mallin had witnessed similar tactics, utilised effectively, in India in the 1890s, which he had written about in the *Workers' Republic*. Clearly, the failure or inability to capture the surrounding buildings meant that any action taken inside the Green was doomed. However, if orders were to seize the Green itself was there much else that Mallin could have done to secure the large, open park he was assigned to? Was Mallin simply guilty of following orders too directly, even when they were certain to fail? Without a detailed record of the plan for the Rising it is impossible to say. Nevertheless, the digging of trenches must be viewed as an attempt, albeit one that failed quite comprehensively, to adapt to the landscape, conditions and difficulties faced by the garrison.

The most infamous aspect of Mallin's Rising is the decision not to occupy, or attempt to occupy, the Shelbourne Hotel. In *The Easter Rebellion* Max Caulfield wrote, 'For all his reputed skill and experience, Mallin made no attempt to take the Shelbourne, though it was easily the most prominent building in the Green, and by virtue of its height, certainly the most commanding.'[19] Historians Barton and Foy have described this as 'a critical and surprising tactical blunder'.[20] Laurence Nugent, who witnessed much of the fighting, believed that

> ... the men from the College of Surgeons could easily have
> captured the few officers who occupied the Shelbourne

Hotel and the Conservative Club. By doing this they would have been free to move at will through a large part of the city. Capt. Cullen and myself, along with members of our deputation, were able to walk up Merrion St and along Stephen's Green to the Mansion House up to and including Friday without any opposition. I am in no way criticising, merely pointing out the position as we saw it. The College of Surgeons, Jacob's or Marrowbone Lane were not attacked at any time during the fight.[21]

Some of those involved again cite a lack of numbers as the reason for the failure to occupy the hotel. Frank Robbins believes the original plan stipulated that Lieutenant George Norgrove and fifty men were due to take the Shelbourne but this plan was dropped at 'the last moment' and Norgrove was detailed to Dublin Castle. He makes no mention of who made this decision.[22] Thomas O'Donoghue has claimed that a Sergeant Keogh was due to occupy the Shelbourne with twelve men under O'Donoghue's command.[23] These accounts suggest that the Shelbourne was part of the original occupation plan, although they do not agree on how this was to be achieved. R.M. Fox's narrative, based largely on the evidence of men who took part in the fighting, including James O'Shea, points to a shortage of manpower resulting from Eoin MacNeill's countermanding order as the reason behind the failure to defend Stephen's Green.[24] This argument does not convince Charles Townshend, and he notes:

The reason usually given for the failure to occupy the Shelbourne, lack of numbers, seems unconvincing… The ICA
had not been affected by the countermanding order, and
turned out pretty much in full strength at Liberty Hall.
Unless a last-minute decision was made to divert men to
the GPO, it is hard to see how any original plan could have
supposed that Mallin would have had a larger force than he
did. If such a decision was made, it proved a costly one.[25]

The accounts of Robbins, O'Shea and O'Donoghue
were all recorded with the considerable benefit of hindsight.
Their accounts, written many years later, may be subject
to the passing of time and the failings of memory as well
as the desire to vindicate their leaders. This makes it difficult to establish whether it was circumstances and a lack of
resources that dictated the decision, or whether it was simply
a momentous 'blunder'. It is likely that it was intended, at
least at some point, to take the Shelbourne. The decision not
to, for whatever reason, remains a surprising one, even from
the perspective that the Shelbourne would have provided a
ready supply of food, beds and other essentials, essentials not
be found in the College of Surgeons, which was occupied
on Easter Monday. It seems to have been discussed on Easter
Monday: Thomas O'Donoghue claims he asked Mallin if
they should take the Shelbourne Hotel 'as there would be
no difficulty holding it with very few men once it was barricaded at the bottom. We would have a source of food supply,

a good position, and eliminate a grave danger to the Green'. Mallin's response was, 'Don't trouble about it.'[26] It may well, as O'Donoghue pointed out, have taken a very small force to seize the building but, perhaps, a much larger force to maintain it, which may explain Mallin's reply. When Liam Ó Briain was asked where he thought the incessant machine-gun fire was coming from he replied, 'from the Shelbourne and the [United Services] Club, I think', and recalls that Mallin, perhaps tellingly, 'nodded his head without speaking'.[27] By that point, the opportunity to occupy the hotel had gone. It proved a costly decision and Mallin and the garrison seem to have realised this quite quickly. It was the machine-gun fire from the hotel that forced the retreat on Tuesday. This, somewhat ironically, also made the trenches, dug throughout Monday, redundant.

Barton and Foy as well as Townshend have been critical of Mallin's organisation of his men, and keen to point out the confusion among the men. According to Barton and Foy, 'Confrontations were made more probable by poor barricade construction. This tempted motorists to drive around or even through the barriers and Mallin's garrison does not appear to have received clear instructions on how to respond.' (Townshend agrees but argues that this was common to the experience in the other garrisons).[28] Similarly, Townshend points to the fact that Liam Ó Briain and Laurence Nugent seem to have been confused by Mallin's decision to evacuate some of the garrison's outposts as no attack had yet been made on them.[29] Nugent witnessed much of the action during the Rising as he travelled in and out of the city and also noted that in the College of Surgeons the 'scouting, if any, seemed defective.'[30] The inexperience and, in many cases, youth of Mallin's garrison can be seen as part of an explanation of these apparent weaknesses but, as leader, some of the blame must rest with Mallin. These weaknesses are surprising when Mallin's performance as Chief-of-Staff in the ICA is taken into account. Militarily, Mallin was one of the most experienced of the leaders having spent over thirteen years in the British army, although he had never held a high rank or commanded men in battle. Barton and Foy have claimed: 'The operation [of seizing Stephen's Green] showed a limited understanding of the nature of urban warfare, but in mitigation it should be remembered that Mallin was functioning under the considerable constraint of an unforeseen and acute lack of manpower.'[31] But Mallin did have a detailed understanding of urban warfare, in theory at least, as evidenced by his articles in the *Workers' Republic*. During the Rising, however, he does not seem to have followed his own outline for successful guerrilla warfare. The method of fighting from rooftops and retreating down small paths and lanes when attacked, emphasised so convincingly by Mallin, is conspicuous by its absence during the rebellion. Again, whether this was Mallin's responsibility or the orders of superiors in not entirely clear. In Richmond barracks after the surrender, Liam Ó Briain recalls a conversation he had with Mallin: Mallin told him that when he was given the plans for the Rising he immediately said, 'Where is the alternative plan for use when this one breaks down? This plan is far too clockwork and there should be an alternative plan.' He was critical of the way all the forces were to 'dovetail' into one another.[32] If this conversation is accurate, it suggests that Mallin did, in fact, carry out the plan as arranged despite his own reservations. Further evidence of this comes from a letter from Séamus Mallin to the *Irish Press* in which he claimed he had in his possession 'some rough notes in pencil, written by my father, in which he sketched out the proposed disposition of the Irish forces in Dublin. These notes were made some time before 1916.' These notes must not have tallied with what actually took place in 1916 as he remarks, 'The recommendations contained in them were not, of course, put into effect.'[33] Unfortunately, these notes have not survived, so it is impossible to say what Mallin's approach to the seizure of Dublin would have been had his recommendations been followed.

Mallin was knowledgeable on the theory behind urban warfare, but the reality of the conflict, and indeed the lack of manpower, proved a difficult challenge for him and some of the shortcomings evident during Easter Week were his responsibility. It may have simply been the case that Mallin felt unable to carry out in practice, or felt those men under his command were unable to carry out in practice, the theory that he had written and spoken about.

What then, of Mallin's individual performance during the fighting, and the reaction of those under his command? The comments of those under Mallin's command are entirely positive. While it is, unsurprisingly, almost impossible to find negative comments from veterans about any executed leader, one should not disregard the commentaries of these veterans. Madeleine ffrench-Mullen, an ICA member who had served as a first-aid officer in the College of Surgeons, wrote the following in the diary she kept while imprisoned after the Rising:

> The Commandant M. Mallin I hardly knew by sight that Easter Monday when I was placed under his command but at the end of the week I knew him better than many life acquaintances. I don't know what struck me most about the man, perhaps his wonderful patience and self-control. I have known him long hours without either food or sleep and yet he would never show the slightest sign of irritation under the most exasperating circumstances. He thought of everyone and everything not merely the important matters but little details as regards our comforts that few men would even think of.[34]

An even more remarkable comment came later:

By the shooting of Mallin and Pearse the English have done us an almost irreparable injury, of the two I would say Mallin was the greatest loss to the country every decade has produced a host of polititians [sic] but our military leaders have been very few and Mallin was the man we needed to organize our Republican Army.[35]

While these comments were still written under the euphoria of the recently defeated Rising they are, none-theless, significant. They clearly show that ffrench-Mullen rated Mallin's military performance and leadership highly. Her first comment also emphasises aspects of Mallin's lead-ership that may go unnoticed by military historians but would be felt strongly by those under his command: con-trol, compassion and kindness. Many years after the Rising, Liam Ó Briain, unfamiliar with Mallin until he somewhat accidentally found himself part of the Stephen's Green gar-rison, described Mallin as 'that wonderful, intensely patri-otic, deeply religious little man, whom I only knew for a fortnight but who left a deeper impression on me than any man I ever met, save Arthur Griffith.'[36] Mallin, in Ó Bri-ain's words, 'seemed to be visiting his posts unceasingly' during the week and also showed considerable humanity for those under his command. Margaret Skinnider remembered how 'gentle and concerned he was when I was so ill in the College of Surgeons' after she had been badly wounded.[37] During the evacuation of Stephen's Green, Mallin refused to leave until he was sure everyone was accounted for and he was one of the last to leave.[38] He received a bullet hole in his hat while rushing out amid gunfire to rescue an injured ICA member.[39] Both Mallin and Markievicz also took part in dangerous excursions to the garrison's outposts during the week.[40]

A number of accounts suggest that, despite Foy and Barton's claim that Mallin was 'unimaginative', he made significant attempts to counteract the British snipers and machine gunners located in prominent buildings around the Green, with varying levels of success. On Wednesday a group of twenty men, under Thomas O'Donoghue, were ordered to threaten British forces at the rear of the Russell Hotel through a number of houses in Harcourt Street. If they were unable to hold out, they were ordered to set fire to the buildings and retreat. As the men were fired on, they were in fact forced to burn the buildings and retreat. It was on this operation that Fred Ryan was killed and Margaret Skinnider wounded.[41] Similarly, Mallin planned to take out machine guns located in the United Services Club and other British posts in the Grafton Street area by tunnelling from the College of Surgeons to Grafton Street. A huge effort was expended by the men engaged in this task, ultimately without success. James O'Shea claims this plan failed, 'not through any fault of Mallin but through a man in charge of the post which was to provide covering

fire. He started firing too soon'.[42] However, Barton and
Foy have stated that this plan was 'completely unrealistic'
due to the increasing British presence and their superior
weaponry. Furthermore, over fifty properties had to be tun-
nelled through with a shortage of men and of adequate
equipment. Nevertheless, this shows that a serious attempt
was made to deal with British fire from this area (one of
their main causes of trouble) and their failure was at times
more due to a lack of experience, manpower and perhaps
luck, than to a lack of initiative.

Despite his military experience and study of guerrilla
warfare, the Easter Rising put Mallin in an unfamiliar situation. While he understood the nature of urban warfare, the
Rising presented situations that Mallin had no experience
of in practice, and a shortage of manpower and resources
was undoubtedly significant. Mallin suffered many of the
same problems as the other garrisons and was no more successful in dealing with them than the other leaders were.
Certainly, errors of judgement were made during the week,
but these should, perhaps, be judged in the context of the
very unique set of circumstances. As Charles Townshend
has pointed out:

> The rebels who went out to do battle on Easter Monday
> morning may have been marching into the unknown, but
> they shared one expectation: that the British military response
> would be rapid and hard. This may have influenced their

choice of positions and procedures in a way that cannot be exactly clarified.

Townshend does, however, add that this assumption was 'the result of a surprising ignorance of the strength and location of the British forces'.[43]

Tactics aside, Mallin's own individual performance, under immense strain, was impressive. As described above, during the week Mallin made a strong impression and elicited much praise from those under his command and comments such as those by Madeleine ffrench-Mullen, Liam Ó Briain and others testify to this.

Chapter 11

After 1916

The Mallin Family;
Commemoration

When her husband was executed, Agnes Mallin was left to deal with the shock of this sudden, unexpected event and the prospect of caring for her young family alone. In May 1916 her eldest was only twelve and she was pregnant with another. Maura Constance Mallin was born on 19 August 1916, 103 days after her father's execution. Maura was baptised among exalted company. William Partridge was asked to become her godfather and gratefully accepted. Countess Markievicz requested the honour of godmother and this was duly granted. Like Partridge, Markievicz was still in prison and Lillie Connolly, James Connolly's widow, served as proxy at the christening. The execution of the rebel leaders had dragged out over nine days, and stories such as the marriage of Grace Gifford to Joseph Plunkett in

Kilmainham Gaol hours before his execution, and the plight of James Connolly, seriously wounded and shot in a chair, had served to create a swell of support for the rebels in a city that had previously jeered and threatened.

This support was not immediately felt by Agnes Mallin, however. While she was in the Coombe hospital giving birth to her daughter, there were protests outside the hospital from some who remained unfavourable to the rebels and their cause.[1] The wives and children left behind by the men executed in May 1916 (and of those killed in battle) have been regularly neglected by historiography. How widows coped with the sudden and tragic loss of a husband and breadwinner and how children grew up with the legacy of a martyred father, who in many cases they never really knew, are aspects of the history of the Rising that are rarely explored.

When Mallin became intricately involved in the plans for revolution the possibility that the revolution would leave his family without a breadwinner must have been difficult to ignore. Frank Robbins recalls that Mallin brought a loom into a workroom in Liberty Hall and began weaving a square of fabric in the hope that his wife might be able to sell it for £10 after the Rising had begun.[2] The perilous financial position in which Mallin left his family is also something that troubled him considerably in his final hours. He did, however, recognise that there would be some support available in the aftermath of the rebellion; his letter to his wife

and appeal to Alderman and member of Dublin Corporation
Thomas Kelly emphasise this.

Almost immediately after the Rising a number of groups
were formed to raise and distribute aid to those who were
afflicted financially by the Rising. On 18 May the Irish
National Aid Association was established 'to effect coopera-
tion amongst four different Committees which had been
formed to relieve those who had suffered as a result of the
rising of the previous month.' An executive including Louise
Gavan Duffy, Michael Davitt, Lorcan Sherlock and Father
Flanagan was appointed. Four representatives from the
Dublin Trades Council (Thomas Farren, William McPartlin,
John Lawlor and Daniel Magee) were appointed, thus allowing members of the Irish Citizen Army to fall under the remit
of the association.[3] The Irish National Volunteer Dependants Fund had also been founded by Áine Ceannt, Kathleen Clarke and Sorcha MacMahon for the same purpose. It
soon became apparent that having two organisations working towards the same aim was impractical. At a conference of
delegates from both groups, held in Dublin's Gresham Hotel
on 11 August 1916, it was decided to amalgamate the elected
executive committees of the Irish National Aid Association
and the Irish National Volunteer Dependants Fund to form
the cumbersomely titled Irish National Volunteer Aid Association Dependants Fund (INVAADF). At its first meeting
on 15 August a new constitution was adopted outlining that:

The objects of the Association are to make adequate provision for the families and dependants of the men who were executed, of those who fell in action, and of those who were sentenced to penal servitude in connection with the Insurrection of Easter, 1916; And, in addition, to provide for the necessities of those others who suffered by reason of participation or suspicion of participation in the Insurrection.[4]

The INVAADF coordinated the collection and distribution of funds in Ireland and also managed money raised in the US through the American Relief Fund. At the 22 April executive meeting a new education sub-committee was formed to replace one previously created by the Irish National Aid Association. This sub-committee included P.T. Keohane (editor of the *Catholic Bulletin* and INVAADF chairman), Thomas Farren and Father Flanagan and was appointed 'to report on and arrange for the education of the children of men executed, killed in the Rising, or sent to penal servitude'. The following week a resolution was passed requiring:

That the Executive directs the Schools Sub-Committee to prepare a list of the children (both boys and girls) of the men executed, killed in action, sentenced to penal servitude, deported, or victimised, with a view to knowing the number of cases to be dealt with. That in the case of the

boys, as St Enda's College, being a memorial to and a con-
tinuation of the work of the late Mr Pearse, is worthy of
support ... as many boys as possible should be selected for
education there, for whose fees, when necessary, the Fund
should be responsible.

On 26 September it was announced that Mallin's eldest
sons, James (Séamus) and John (Seán), had been entered at St
Enda's.[5] They were joined by Thomas Clarke's eldest son and
Éamonn Ceannt's son, Rónán.

At the 12 September executive meeting, P.T. Keohane
raised the necessity of investigating fully the financial circumstances of the families and dependants of the executed
men and the special grants sub-committee were requested
to begin inquiries. On 10 October the education sub-committee reported on its last meeting at which the education
of the children of the executed was discussed. It was decided
that before the education of any child was finally dealt with
the remaining parent or guardian would be consulted. The
sub-committee further recommended that all dependants
of the executed men should be contacted to ascertain their
circumstances. Following this recommendation the recently
defunct American fund sub-committee, which had included
Jennie Wyse Power and Sorcha MacMahon, was reappointed
to 'inquire into and report on the circumstances of the families of the men executed, killed in action or sent to penal
servitude.' It was further decided to draft a letter to be sent to

each of the families in question, along with a return envelope to be addressed to the chairman, P.T. Keohane. Following its enquiries the sub-committee produced a document outlining the financial situation of the families of those executed and killed in action. It listed their income, both prior to and after the rebellion, aid already received, the dependant's suggestions, the sub-committee's comments and the recommended grant. The sums outlined were passed by the executive on 10 December, but it was unanimously agreed that the sums passed:

> should be regarded as the minimum, with the possibility of increase later on if the funds permitted; also that the Treasurers should transfer the total amounts recommended and passed to a separated deposit a/c and that the interest on that account should be allowed to accumulate for the additional benefit of the families for whom the amounts so deposited were ear-marked.

Any permanent investments of the funds were to be considered by the sub-committee before any further investment was made.[6]

The document showing the assessment carried out by the American grants (extended) sub-committee, seven months after the Rising, is fascinating. It emphasises the vast differences in the circumstances of the executed men as well and how the social class of a family could determine how much relief they received. Mallin's prior income is recorded as a paltry £2.10.0, while in contrast Thomas MacDonagh's was over £350 and Éamonn Ceannt's £220, firmly placing them in the middle class. Only James Connolly (£3 plus £2.8.0 from his daughter), Michael O'Hanrahan (£6), and Con Colbert, who taught at St Enda's, ('Just sufficient for himself') seem to have had such small incomes. O'Hanrahan and Colbert were, however, unmarried and had no children. By the time the report was compiled, Agnes Mallin had earned no income but was given £100 from the American Relief Fund and was in receipt of a weekly grant of £1.7.0 from the INVAADF. The school fees of Séamus and Seán Mallin were also covered. When asked for recommendations it seems not all dependants offered any, but Agnes requested an increase of the grant for clothes. She was also concerned about the education of her children and wished to know more definitely about their situation. Thomas Farren interviewed Agnes and he considered it 'most advisable' that the weekly grant be continued and that the fund should look after the children's education. A grant of £1000, a considerable sum of money at the time, was recommended and it was decided to invest this on the family's behalf with the interest defrayed against the cost of educating the children.[7] Some of the dependants of Irish Volunteer leaders were given money by the Irish Volunteer Dependants Fund. James Connolly's widow was allocated £50.

The American Relief Fund money was distributed to the executed leader's dependants in a manner that reflected their social standing prior to the Rising. Mallin's wife and five children received £100 while Con Colbert's ill sister received £150. Thomas MacDonagh's wife, Muriel Gifford, received £500 alogether from the Irish Volunteer Dependants Fund and the American Relief Fund.[8] It must also be noted that the dependants of those killed in action received substantially lower amounts of aid. Richard O'Carroll, who was shot during the Rising and later died of his wounds, left a wife and seven children – his dependants were allocated a smaller amount than those of the executed men. Executed men were put in a higher category than those killed in action.

A photograph of the Mallin family appeared in the December 1916 edition of the *Catholic Bulletin*, along with the families of some of the other deceased men. They were published as part of a drive to raise funds for the 'education of the innocent children thus left to the care and sympathy of nationalist Ireland.' All monies donated were to be passed by the *Catholic Bulletin* to the education sub-committee of the INVAADF, and were only to be used to provide for the education of dependants. It was hoped the photographs would further intensify the growing public interest in those left behind after the Rising and 'help to a truer appreciation of the sacrifices involved in the tragic family severances of Easter Week'.[9]

P.T. Keohane, editor of the *Catholic Bulletin* and chairman of the INVAADF, provided much support to the Mallin family. A benefactor in the US, who wished to remain anonymous, offered to pay for the education of two sons of the 'fallen' through the *Catholic Bulletin* and the INVAADF. The decision was left to Keohane, who chose Séamus and Seán Mallin. Both were sent to St Enda's, then to Knockbeg College, a Dublin boarding school.[10] In June 1917 the INDAAVF decided to arrange a seaside holiday for some of the children of those killed during the Rising and a committee was established to make arrangements. On 19 June it was announced that a two-month holiday had been organised for Agnes Mallin and her children, along with fellow trade unionist Richard O'Carroll's widow and children.[11]

In 1924 the Military Pensions Service Act was introduced to provide military pensions for those who had active service in the Irish Volunteers (later the Irish Republican Army) and the Citizen Army from 1916 to 1921. Many of those who had been opposed to the Anglo-Irish Treaty, and subsequently fought on the anti-Treaty side during the Civil War refused to accept pensions or did not apply to the scheme. The Act was amended in 1934, under the Éamon de Valera-led Fianna Fáil government, to allow those who had not received a pension under the previous Act to apply. Under the 1924 Act, Agnes Mallin was given an allowance of thirty shillings per week, a reduced amount as Michael Mallin had not signed the Proclamation. Joseph Mallin recalls that his mother had meetings with W.T. Cosgrave, leader of the Cumann na nGaedhael government, and Seán T. O'Kelly, later President of Ireland, about the matter: 'I sensed a feeling of hurt in my mother after her meeting with W Cosgrave. The one with Sean T was much more compassionate. Nothing resulted.'[12]

Those who knew Mallin and had fought with him during Easter Week were acutely aware of the position of his family following his death. William Partridge expressed his concern in a letter to his wife from Lewes prison: 'I hope Mrs Mallin has regained her strength – as I know she will bear her cross.'[13] While in Mountjoy prison, Countess Markievicz seems to have asked her sister Eva to locate Agnes and wrote, 'I hope you found Mrs Mallin. I wish I knew, for it worries me so to think of her.'[14] Markievicz possibly offered money to the family which was prevented entirely or eventually stopped, as in September 1916, writing to her sister from Aylesbury prison, Markievicz expressed the hope that 'Mrs M[allin] is getting her £1 alright and can do without my 10/-.'[15] In February 1917 Markievicz received an update about the Mallin family and in her reply showed that she was still aware of the loss Agnes had suffered:

> I was glad to hear of Mrs M[allin], and so interested to learn that the boy is learning to draw. Perhaps I shall be able to help him, some day. Who knows? ... It would probably upset

Mrs M[allin] very much, seeing me. It would bring it all back to her. They were such a devoted pair. The last things he said to me were about her.[16]

Following the Rising, the Mallins remained in their home at Emmet Hall for a number of years. The house was raided on several occasions by British forces. During one raid Agnes coolly covered her husband's ceremonial sword with newspapers as the armed soldiers burst through the door. The raiders took Agnes Mallin's bank book and a pair of night glasses and other items given to Mallin by James Connolly. After Agnes reported this to the barracks next door, the bank book was returned, but none of the other items taken. Joseph Mallin has vivid memories of a raid on Armistice Day 1918, when Great War hostilities ceased. Soldiers, probably intoxicated, entered the building and the family were forced to flee.[17]

Under the auspices of the INVAADF the property of a number of those who suffered a loss as a result of the Rising was placed under trust deeds. These deeds meant that in return for a cash loan the property was placed in the hands of a trustee. The Mallin home, Emmet Hall in Inchicore, was put under trust deed. The property was valued at £2,868.17.1 and a cash loan was received to the amount of £23.13.1. Thomas Farren and Rose Nolan became trustees on the property.[18] In 1924 the family left Emmet Road. With the help of Thomas Farren a home was found in Mount Brown, where rent of ten shillings per week was paid.

The shock of her husband's death seems to have directly affected Agnes Mallin's health. Further, despite the aid provided to the family, Agnes returned to work. It is not clear why she decided to do this. Through the relief fund her children were being educated to a level that would have been out of reach for the family prior to the rebellion; they had also received substantial amounts of money from the INVAADF and the White Cross. While they were by no means able to afford an extravagant lifestyle, it may not have been necessary for Agnes to return to work to provide for her family. Perhaps she wanted a sense of purpose or feared that the aid money would run out? She had worked as a nurse prior to her marriage and took a job as a night nurse in the South Dublin Union (now St James's hospital). She also worked as a school attendance officer. In 1924 she contracted tuberculosis. That year, too, a surgeon performed an operation removing bone from a shin bone to be placed in her spine. A year of bed rest followed the operation, which meant that Agnes was unable to look after her youngest child, Maura, then eight years old. By that time Joseph Mallin was a pupil in St Enda's and in September 1924 Margaret Pearse, sister of Patrick, who was living and working at St Enda's, wrote to Agnes offering to look after Maura while Agnes was ill:

It would be an honour to help you over this time of trouble. She would have her meals with us, we would look after her in every way, she could have lots of milk & fresh air, &

go to school every day to the convent ... In the evenings
I would prepare your little one for first Confession & first
Communion, as she is already a year over age. She would
play with Joseph too in the evenings but she would not
mix with the other boys except the babies. ...There are two
pious ladies in Rathfarnham who are hoping the little one
may come.[19]

Maura's first communion was celebrated on the first day
her mother was allowed out of bed.[20] Joseph Mallin recalls
overhearing the surgeon speaking to another doctor and
attributing Agnes's illness 'directly' to the strain of 1916. She
made a full recovery but in 1929 the tuberculosis returned.
Agnes was cared for in a home in Dún Laoghaire for a
period. There her 'deep concern and consideration for the
other patients expressed a selflessness' that drew the respect
and admiration of the chaplain. It was felt that another operation might be more than she could bear and it was decided
that home care would be of greater benefit. Through Joe
Connolly and Mrs Barrett (brother and sister of Seán Connolly) an ambulance was provided to transport Agnes home.
Margaret Pearse arranged for a woman who had worked in
St Enda's to move into the family home to provide care.
Michael Mallin's sister, Katie, paid weekly visits as did Dr
David White. Joseph Mallin had finished school by now
and was able to offer care and companionship as his moth-
er's health worsened. Agnes died on 2 May 1932. Her son

Séamus, who had been working in Venezuela, was travelling and it was impossible to contact him until a month after his mother's death.[21] The *Catholic Bulletin* published a short obituary piece in its 'Gleanings' column:

> Mrs Mallin, who belonged to a Dublin family of fine repute, was the worthy wife of one of the martyred heroes of the Rising; and, in God's design, they are survived by a family that are a credit to Irish parenthood. Taking them in order of their age, Séamus has become a brilliant engineer in Venezuela; Seán an equally promising member of the society of Jesus; Una a nun in Spain. Readers of the BULLETIN will recall the last wish of the sentenced father that their baby Joe should become a priest. Joe and Máire, the younger members of the family, grew up to be the consolation of their devoted mother through the long illness that ended in her death, and both give promise of creditably responding to the dearest wishes and highest hopes of their valiant parents.[22]

In an article in the *Irish Times* in 1991, Maura Mallin spoke of her memories of her mother, noting, 'Her life really was a very sad and trying one', but also 'I remember her as the most wonderful person in the world. I never remember her making our lives remotely unhappy. Not that she wasn't sad – she *was*.'[23] Similarly, Joseph has noted that his mother was wise and prudent. She never spoke of her husband in order to allow her children grow up without the burden of his memory.[24]

Two of Mallin's younger brothers followed his example and were active members of the IRA during the War of Independence from 1919 to 1921. John Mallin was a member of C Company, Third Battalion of the Dublin Brigade who were active around the Camden Street area of the city. He was imprisoned for a period and while in Wormwood Scrubs prison in London took part in a twenty-four day hunger strike. Bart was also a member of C Company and though wounded several times, once in Camden Street by a grenade thrown from a lorry carrying British forces, he was never arrested.[25]

It is Séamus Mallin, the eldest of Michael Mallin's children, who had the most vivid recollections of his father. The most obvious influence of his father's execution on his life was his decision to oppose the Anglo-Irish Treaty, signed in December 1921. Following the Treaty split, Séamus, though still only in his teens, joined the anti-Treaty IRA. On 23 October 1922, he was arrested by Free State forces and found to be in possession of a rifle. Tried on 11 November 1922, he was found guilty of 'having possession without proper authority of a revolver' and sentenced to five years' penal servitude.[26] The Public Safety Resolution, introduced in September 1922, had made the unauthorised possession of a rifle a capital offence; Séamus Mallin faced the real prospect of execution, something his mother would have been very aware of, though she did not pass on any of her worry or anxiety to the rest of the family. In this case, his father's name may have helped to save Séamus from that fate – executing the son of a 1916 leader would have offered an opportunity for powerful anti-Free State propaganda. Séamus was interned for two and a half years in total and joined other anti-Treaty prisoners in the Curragh on a hunger strike in 1923 which lasted thirty days before it was called off.[27]

Following his release, he resumed the engineering studies in University College Dublin that had been interrupted by his internment. He graduated in 1926 and his first employment came with the Shannon scheme. The Shannon scheme was an initiative of the first Free State government led by the pro-Treaty Cumann na nGaedhal. That Séamus was employed on this scheme is interesting considering his very recent anti-Treaty leanings. Soon after his work on the Shannon scheme was completed, he took up a position in Venezuela. When that contract expired he spent some time travelling in South America; his mother passed away at this time. In 1932 Séamus returned to Dublin to work for the Dublin County Council. It seems that Laurence Kettle, an electrical engineer with the council and a prisoner of the Stephen's Green garrison in 1916, was influential in securing this job.[28] In 1939, having worked with the Irish Sugar Company and the Dublin Port Milling Company, he began work with the engineering department of the Office of Public Works. In 1945 he moved to the Fisheries Division of the Department of Agriculture, later becoming its head engineer where he remained until his retirement in 1969.

Séamus Mallin had a distinguished career in the fisheries industry. He was appointed chairman of the Irish Sea Fisheries Association and when this body was replaced by Bord Iascaigh Mhara in 1952 he became its first chairman, holding the post until 1962. Following his retirement from the Department of Agriculture he was retained as an advisor to the Irish deputation at the United Nations Law of the Sea Conference and carried out his consultancy position with energy and vigour. He married and had two sons, Michael and Seán, and three daughters, Germaine, Una and Anete. He died, aged seventy-eight, in 1982. An obituary in the *Irish Times* reflected on how Séamus Mallin lived with his father's legacy:

> he was too full of the joy of life to wallow in the patriotism of martyrology. Instead he lived for his country as his father died for it. ... Generous as a host he was also generous of mind. He transcended the tragedy of his father's death and, while remaining loyal to Gaelic Ireland, was appreciative of different traditions of Irish life about him.[29]

Seán Mallin decided to join the Society of Jesus, the Jesuits. He spent much of his life working in county Galway.

Seán Mallin died on 3 January 1977, the first of the Mallin children to pass away.

Michael Mallin had requested that his daughter Una, then aged four, become a nun. It is that request, above all else, that dictated the influence her father's legacy would have on his eldest daughter. Una Mallin joined the Loreto order in 1925. She travelled to Spain in the 1920s and spent the rest of her life living and working there. She had been due to return to Ireland in the 1980s, but suffered a stroke and died.

Mallin wished for two of his offspring to join 'the service of God' and also requested his youngest son to join the priesthood. It was not until his mother's death in 1932 that Joseph Mallin decided to fulfil his father's wish; like his brother he joined the Jesuits. No mention had ever been made on the subject by his mother. He had finished his education in St Enda's in 1931 and, following her death, Joseph spent some time living in the home of Austin Stack (where he was taught to play bridge by Seán Russell).[30] In 1938 he decided to live and work as a missionary in China where he eventually found himself in an administrative role and was involved in the foundation of a primary school in Hong Kong. With the death of his sister, Maura, in 2005, Joseph Mallin became the last surviving offspring of the executed leaders of the Rising.

Like Joseph, who was only two and a half years old when his father was executed, Maura Mallin, who was born after

his execution, had no direct memories of her father. Maura
was fourteen years old when her mother died. It was she
and Joseph who had been closest to their mother during
her illness. Maura then went to the Loreto convent in Bray,
County Wicklow, as a boarder and having finished her studies travelled to Spain, spending a number of years in Bar-
celona and becoming fluent in Spanish. She retained many
Spanish friends for the rest of her life. Having returned to
Ireland, Maura met Bob Phillips and was married in 1944.
The couple had two sons, David (b. 1946) and Michael (b.
1949). In the 1960s Bob Phillips suffered an accident and was
brain damaged and crippled. After a spell in hospital, he was
cared for by his wife until his death in 1986. Maura's own
final years were spent in hospital. She died on 20 April 2005
in Our Lady's Hospice, Harold's Cross, Dublin. According to
Joseph Mallin, Maura always refused any compensation or
privilege from the state, believing it would 'demean 1916'.[31]
In an interview with John Waters for the *Irish Times* in 1991,
Maura Phillips reflected on the Rising and her father:

> …Maura is unhappy with the way the tradition of the Rising
> has been usurped by the Provisional IRA. She believes we
> should not allow this to prevent us marking the 75th [anni-
> versary] in a full and proper manner. 'But I would prefer the
> word "commemoration" to "celebration",' she says. 'I know
> a lot of people would think now it was a mistake. But who
> am I to say that? According to what my mother told me,

my father did not go out presuming they were going to lose and he was going to die. That might have been in Pearse's mind, but it was certainly not in my father's.'[32]

Michael Mallin's children followed very different paths in their adult lives. Each lived with the loss of a father in their own way. In his youth, Séamus followed his father in bearing arms for the republic (albeit in a much less dramatic fashion) but in adulthood lived the life of a well-respected and popular civil servant. Séamus and Maura married and raised families. Seán and Joseph became Jesuit priests and Una a Loreto nun. Foreign travel was the one shared experience in their lives. One could attribute this to a desire to 'escape' the Irish obsession with the history of the Rising or simply an inherited lust for adventure and new experiences. The latter seems more probable. The death and legacy of their father was inescapable for the Mallin children. Growing up without a father in itself had its effect on each of them. Mallin's powerful last letter influenced the career paths of two of his children, but the decision to serve abroad offered an opportunity to have experiences not available in Ireland. Agnes Mallin's decision not to share much about their father with her youngest children perhaps saved her from the pain of recollection, but also meant they grew up not missing a father they had never known.

Commemoration

The commemoration of the Rising and those who had died was a divisive affair, particularly in the 1930s and 1940s. The split in the Sinn Féin movement that followed the Civil War meant that many who had fought side by side in 1916 had become bitter political opponents. The first official state commemoration of the Rising took place at the grave of the executed leaders in Arbour Hill in April 1924. It was, necessarily, a rather low-key affair, but invitations were sent to the relatives of all the executed men. Letters of thanks were received from most, refusals from others, but Agnes Mallin was the only relative to attend. It was 'no surprise that Mrs Mallin was on her own, given the political affiliations of the other relatives, who were avowedly republican and hostile to the ruling government.'[33] It is nonetheless worthy of note that Agnes did attend. While there is no evidence that she actively opposed the Treaty, or had any interest in it at all, other members of the family did. Séamus, her eldest son, was interned in the Curragh for his anti-Treaty IRA activity and uncles of his were also IRA members. It seems in this case, that Agnes's wish to remember her husband outweighed political convictions.

Seventeen years after his mother attended the first official state commemoration, Séamus Mallin was forced to write to the Department of the Taoiseach to point out that he had never received an invitation for the annual event; 1941

225

was the twenty-fifth anniversary of the Rising and Séamus had yet to visit his father's grave. P.J. Long, secretary to the Department of Defence confirmed that he was not on the official list for invitations. The list, however, had not been updated for the previous eight years, save additions. The list stated that Michael Mallin's next-of-kin were his father John Mallin and his brother Thomas Mallin, who had each been sent invitations to all of the previous ceremonies. Whether this was a simple piece of administrative oversight or something more sinister (perhaps related to Séamus's IRA past) is not clear. Regardless, he was informed that he would receive an invitation to all future ceremonies.[34] This was not the last time a government would overlook a member of the Mallin family at the time of an official commemoration. In 2006, Fr Joseph Mallin, based in Hong Kong, received an invitation to the ninetieth anniversary celebrations only after correspondence from relatives to the Taoiseach.

Like the other 1916 leaders, Mallin's name has been remembered through the naming of streets, buildings and railway stations in the first fifty years of the Free State. Dún Laoghaire railway station officially became Dún Laoghaire/Mallin station, though this title is rarely, if ever, used. Michael Mallin House was built close to Mallin's old home in Meath Street. There is now a Mallin Avenue in Dublin 8; Back Lane in Wexford became Mallin Lane in 1920. More unusually, there is now a Michael Mallin Park in Newry, County

Down, located close to James Connolly Park. In November 2011, a plaque was unveiled by the Kilmainham and Inchicore Historical Society, funded by the trade union SIPTU, on 122 Emmet Road (Emmet Hall), remembering the building's links with the ITGWU, some of those who frequently visited the building and that it was Mallin's family home.

A letter to the editor of the *Irish Times*, dated 2 November 1966, from Seán Dowling of the Kilmainham Gaol Restoration Society, offers a revealing perspective into the perception of Mallin fifty years after his execution. The letter was in relation to a dispute about the Labour Party's wish to erect a plaque to James Connolly in the stonebreaker's yard of Kilmainham Gaol:

> We in Kilmainham do not forget that Connolly commanded the combined forces of the Republic in Dublin in 1916. Neither do we forget another man who left his young family and pregnant wife to take command of the Irish Citizen Army and go, as he knew, to his death. The Labour Party have not sought to erect a plaque to the memory of Michael Mallin. They have chosen to forget him because he has no political value for them.[35]

Amidst the political scramble for 'ownership' of the legacy of the Rising, culminating in the fiftieth anniversary celebrations in 1966, it is easy to see why the Labour Party would wish to claim James Connolly as their own. Why, though, was

Mallin's name seen to have no 'political value' by this time? Figures and stories who captured the public imagination in the immediate aftermath of the Rising (The O'Rahilly, Richard O'Carroll and Michael Malone's death in Clanwilliam House, for example), have over time faded from popular memory. The names that have endured most strongly are those of Pearse, Connolly and Markievicz. It was, one could argue, Mallin's bad luck that he was so closely associated with two of these, Connolly and Markievicz. Markievicz's sheer force of personality and legacy has played its own role in the sidelining of Mallin's story. A 1917 pamphlet entitled *The Sinn Féin Leaders of 1916* referred to Mallin at the end of a section entitled 'Company Commanders'; Markievicz was given an earlier, longer piece among some of the more important contemporary figures.[36] There may be a sense of inevitability here given the very distinctive personalities of Connolly and Markievicz, but certainly, for Citizen Army veterans the names of Connolly and Mallin always came together. In his book *Under the Starry Plough*, Frank Robbins describes an 'atmosphere entirely different from that moulded by Connolly and Mallin' in the Citizen Army after 1916. He is also critical of the new leadership who, in his opinion, preferred to 'procrastinate rather than to take the line that would have been laid down by Connolly or Mallin, were either there to lead.' Connolly and Mallin shared a vision for the Citizen Army and for Robbins and others, the Citizen Army was a symbol of the vision of both men. When the terms of the Anglo-Irish Treaty were announced in December 1921, Dr Kathleen Lynn wrote in her diary, '"Peace" terms but what a peace! Not what Connolly & Mallin and countless others died for.'[37] A 1924 election poster for future Fianna Fáil Taoiseach Sean Lemass, invoking the writing of James Connolly to appeal to the workers of Dublin, went as follows: 'Sinn Féin has set itself the task of putting the Republic on a sound basis. James Connolly, William Partridge, Dick O'Carroll and Michael Mallin, at the moment of crisis, put the national programme first ... Workers! Will you follow the lead of Connolly, Partridge, O'Carroll and Mallin?'[38] If it had none in 1966, Mallin's name clearly had some value in 1924.

Those who did not sign the Proclamation have generally been the most overlooked of the executed men. It could also be argued that Mallin has been gradually sidelined as he was one of the few committed socialists among the leaders – it was, after all, Citizen Army veterans who were most keen to remember him. Mallin was a quieter, calmer person than either Connolly or Markievicz, two socialist figures whose fame has eclipsed most others; he was also more inclined to organise than orate, and as a result may not have made an immediately obvious icon for the legacy of 1916. Perhaps there was room only for those two great figures in the labour history of the Rising?

Appendix 1

Michael Mallin's last letter to his wife Agnes, Kilmainham Goal, 7 May 1916

[*This is reproduced as in the original, with page breaks indicated in square brackets and underlinings retained.*]

My darling Wife Pulse of my heart, this is the end of all things earthly; sentense of Death has been passed, and a quarter to four tomorrow the sentense will be carried out by shooting and so must Irishmen pay for trying to make Ireland a free nation, Gods will be done. I am prepared but oh my darling if only you and the little ones were coming too if we could all reach Heaven together my heart strings are torne to pieces when I think of you and them of our manly James, happy go lucky John Shy warm Una <u>dadys Girl</u> and oh little Joseph my little man my little man Wife dear Wife I cannot keep the tears back when I think of him he will rest in my arms no more, to think that I have to leave you to battle through the world with them without my help, what will you do my own darling if I had only taken your advice and left the Country we might have been so happy but Ireland

230

always came first, I would ask a special favour of you wife of my heart, but I leave you absolutely free in the matter dont give your love to any other man you are only a girl yet and perhaps it is selfish of me to ask it of you but my darling this past forghtnight has taught me that you are my only love my only hope. I have sinned against you many times in the fulness of your pure holy love for me you will forgive me my many transgressions against you and of our unborne Babe if a Boy call him after me if a Girl after our blessed Lady with Gods help I will be always near you [p.2] If you can I would like you to dedicate Una to the service of God and also Joseph, so that we may have two to rest on as penance for our sins try and do this if you can pray to our Divine Lord that it may be so, Fr McCarty has just been in with me and heard my confession and made me so happy and contented. he will see to the Education and General welfare of our dear ones; you must go and see him my darling Fr McCarty James St God Bless him as well you will go and see Alderman T. Kelly, he is a good God fearing man and will be able to help you for my sake as well as yours he will know what to do, it is due to you as the Wife of one of the fallen, when I left Richmond Barracks to come he (Kilmahainm) the only one of my household that I could cast my longing Eyes on was poor Prinie the <u>dog</u> she looked so faithfull there at the door are you sure you left nothing in the house you know the Police broke in and made a thorough search, however those are mere earthly things let me get back to you and I we have now been married thirteen years or so and in all that time you have been a true loving wife too good for me, you love me my own darling think only of the happy times we spent together forgive and forget all else, I am so cold this has been such a cruel week, Mr Partrige was more than a Brother to me kept me close in his arms so that I might have comfort and warmeth his Wife is here under arrest if he gets out and you see him tell him I met my fate like a man, I do not believe our Blood has been shed in vain. I believe Ireland will come out greater and grander but she must not forget she is <u>Catholic</u> she must keep her Faith. I find no fault with the soldiers or Police I forgive them from the Bottom of my heart, pray for all the souls who fell in this fight Irish & English [p. 3] God and his Blessed mother take you and my dear ones in their care a Husbands Blessing on your dear head my loving Wife a Fathers Blessing on the heads of my children James John Una Joseph my little man, my little man, my little man, his name unnerves me again, all your dear faces arise before me God bless you God bless you my darlings oh if you were only dieing with me but that is sinful. God and his Blessed mother Guard you again and again Pulse of my heart good by for a while, I feel you will soon be in heaven with me if anyone comes to you for any money that I owe them investigate them and so far as lies in your power pay them. I am offering my life as atonment for all my sins and for any debts due but if any debt press undully on any one try and pay them for my sake, give my love to your dear Mother Josephine Mr Farrell Mary-Jane your aunt Julia Mrs Carty and all the children they must all pray for my Poor Soul you will have a mass [p. 4] said for me loved Wife, my life is numbered by hours now darling. I am drawing nearer and nearer to God, to that Good God who died for us, you and I love, and our children, and our childrens children, God and his Blessed Mother again and again Bless and protect you Oh saviour of man if my dear ones could die and enter heaven with me, how Blessed and happy I would they would be away from the cares and trials of the world Una my little one be a <u>Nun</u> Joseph my little man be a Priest if you can James & John to you the care of your mother make yourselves good strong men for her sake Remember <u>Ireland</u> good by my Wife my darling, Remember me, God again Bless and Protect you and our children. I must now Prepare these last few hours must be spent with God alone Your loving Husband Michael Mallin Commandant Stephens Green Command

I enclose the Buttons off my sleeve keep them in memory of me Mike xxxxxx

Appendix 2

Michael Mallin's Last Letter to his father and mother, Kilmainham Gaol, 7 May 1916

My dear Mother and Father,

Forgive your poor son who is soon to meet his death. I am to be shot tomorrow at a quarter to four. Forgive him all his shortcomings towards you – this applies especially in the management of my father's business. Dear father, forgive me all, and you, dear mother, the pain I give you now. Pray for me. Give my love to Tom, May, John, Bart, Katie and Jack Andrews. They must all pray for me. I tried, with others, to make Ireland a free nation and failed. Other failed before us and paid the price and so must we. Good-bye until I meet you in Heaven. Good-bye again. A kiss for you, dear mother. God bless you all. I have now but a few hours left. That I must spend in prayer to God, that good God who died that we might be saved. Give my love to all. Ask Uncle

James to forgive me any pain I may have caused him. Ask Tom Price and all in the trade to forgive me. I forgive all who may have done me harm. God bless them all. Goodbye again Mother dear, and Father, God bless you. Your loving son, Michael Mallin

Piarais MacLochlainn added to following note to his publication of the letter:

A manuscript copy of this letter – not in Mallin's handwriting – is held in the National Library. The original cannot be traced. Although the copy manuscript bears the wrong date – 9th instead of 7th May – and contains some misspellings (corrected in the reproduction) the text has every appearance of authenticity; and Mallin's son, Séamus, confirms that there was such a letter.

Certainly, the use of punctuation and capitals is out of character with Mallin's letter-writing style – he rarely used any punctuation when writing letters – and based on the letter to Mallin's wife it is not unlikely that the original would have contained the misspellings corrected in MacLochlainn's text. The reference to 'my father's business' is a confusing one, but overall the sentiments and tone of the letter, as pointed out by MacLochlainn, do appear authentic.

Notes

Chapter 1:

1 'Events of Easter Week', *Catholic Bulletin*, Vol. VI, No. VII (July 1916), p398.

2 *Sinn Féin Leaders of 1916*, Dublin, 1917.

3 *Inniu*, 30 Oct. 1966.

4 Mallin family 1901 and 1911 census returns (National Archives of Ireland); Bureau of Military History Witness Statement (BMH WS) 382 (Thomas Mallin).

5 Ibid.

6 Fr Joseph Mallin, S.J., to the author, 13 Nov. 2009.

7 *Inniu*, 30 Oct. 1966.

8 *Inniu*, 30 Oct. 1966.

9 BMH WS 382 (Thomas Mallin); Account book of Michael Mallin, Royal Scots Fusiliers (Kilmainham Gaol Archive); Michael Mallin's British army record (National Archives, Kew: WO/97).

Chapter 2:

1 John Buchan, *The History of the Royal Scots Fusiliers 1678-1918*, 1925, p228-9.

2 Ibid, p229.

3 Michael Mallin's British army record (National Archives, Kew: WO 97/5453/27).

4 *Inniu*, 30 Oct. 1966.

5 Michael Mallin's British army record (National Archives, Kew: WO 97/5453/27).

6 Account book of Michael Mallin, Royal Scots Fusiliers (Kilmainham Gaol Archive).

7 Michael Mallin's British army record (National Archives Kew: WO 97/5453/27).

8 Buchan, pp230-1.

9 Buchan, pp232-3.

10 Michael Mallin's British army record (National Archives Kew: WO 97/5453/27).

11 Buchan, pp232-3.

12 These letters were found by Joseph Mallin following his mother's death in 1932. They are currently in the possession of Sinead McCoole. She has kindly allowed the reproduction of the passages quoted in the text.

13 Michael Mallin to Agnes Hickey, 20 Nov. 1897.

14 Michael Mallin to Agnes Hickey, 20 Nov. 1897.

15 Michael Mallin to Agnes Hickey, 18 Nov. 1900.

16 Michael Mallin to Mrs J. Hickey, 2 Oct. 1902 (NLI: Acc 6358).

17 Michael Mallin to Agnes Hickey, 19 Dec. 1897.

18 Michael Mallin to Agnes Hickey, 1 Aug. 1899.

19 Michael Mallin to Agnes Hickey, 21 Mar. 1897.

20 Michael Mallin to Agnes Hickey, 14 Jun. 1901.

21 Michael Mallin to Agnes Hickey, 23 Mar. 1898.

22 Michael Mallin to Agnes Hickey, 19 Apr. 1901.

23 Michael Mallin to Agnes Hickey, 23 Mar. 1898; Ibid, 8 Mar. 1901.

24 *Irish Press*, 8 May 1961.

25 Michael Mallin to Mrs J. Hickey, 25 May 1901 (NLI: Acc 6358).

26 Michael Mallin to Agnes Hickey, 1 Mar. 1898; Ibid, 19 Jun. 1899.

27 Michael Mallin to Mrs J. Hickey, 25 May 1901 (NLI: Acc 6358).

28 Michael Mallin to Agnes Hickey, 18 Oct. 1901.

29 Michael Mallin to Agnes Hickey, 12 Sept. 1902.

30 Michael Mallin to Mrs J Hickey, 3 Oct. 1902 (NLI: Acc: 6358).

31 Michael Mallin to Agnes Hickey, 31 Oct. 1902.

32 Michael Mallin to Agnes Hickey, 21 Nov. 1902.

33 Michael Mallin's British army record (National Archives Kew: WO 97/5453/27).

34 BMH WS 382 (Thomas Mallin). Following his discharge, Mallin was presented with a pocket watch enscribed 'A present from the N.C.Os. and men of the Drums 1st R.S.F. to Dr[ummer] M. Mallin as a token of esteem.' This watch was donated to the Kilmainham Gaol museum by Mallin's son, Fr Joseph Mallin.

35 Michael Mallin to Agnes Hickey, 7 Sep. 1898.

36 Michael Mallin to Agnes Hickey, 14 Nov. 1900.

37 Michael Mallin to Agnes Hickey, 1 Mar. 1898.

38 Michael Mallin to Agnes Hickey, 7 Aug. 1898.

39 Michael Mallin to Agnes Hickey, 24 May 1901.

40 Michael Mallin to Agnes Hickey, 7 Sept. 1898.

41 Michael Mallin to Agnes Hickey, 14 Nov. 1900.

42 Michael Mallin to Agnes Hickey, 21 Sept. 1898.

43 Michael Mallin to Agnes Hickey, 10 May 1901.

44 BMH WS 382 (Thomas Mallin).

45 Michael Mallin to Agnes Hickey, 19 Apr. 1901.

46 *Inniu*, 30 Oct. 1902. Mallin's admission card to the confraternity is preserved in the Kilmainham Gaol museum.

47 BMH WS 6 (Liam Ó Briain).

Chapter 3:

1 Certificate of marriage of Michael Mallin to Agnes Hickey, 26 April 1903 (General Register Office, Dublin).

2 *Catholic Bulletin*, Vol. VI, No. XII (Dec. 1916), p701.

3 *Inniu*, 30 Oct. 1966; Ibid, 7 Nov. 1966. James O'Shea remembers first meeting Mallin in the shop in Capel Street: BMH WS 733 (James O'Shea).

4 BMH WS 382 (Thomas Mallin).

5 *Inniu*, 14 Nov. 1966.

6 Ibid.

7 Breathnach, Katherine, 'The Last of the Dublin Silk Weavers', *Irish Arts Review Yearbook* (1990/1991), p134.

8 Ibid, pp134-7; Campion, Mary, 'An Old Dublin Industry: Poplin', *Dublin Historical Record*, Vol. 19, No. 1 (December 1963), pp2-15.

9 Campion, 'An Old Dublin Industry', p12.

10 For a detailed interview on the life of a Dublin silk weaver at this time see transcript of taped interview with Padraig Breathnach, published in Breathnach, 'The Last of the Dublin Silk Weavers', pp138-143.

11 I am grateful to Francis Devine for the membership figures quoted.

12 Indenture of Bartholomew Mallin into the Dublin silk trade, (Allen Library, Box 200, File A, Pack M).

13 *Irish Press*, 7 Jun. 1935.

14 *The Irish Times*, 1 Nov., 1906; *Evening Herald*, 31 Oct., 1906; *Dublin Evening Mail*, 31 Oct., 1906; *Evening Telegraph*, 31 Oct., 1906.

15 Breathnach, 'Last of the Dublin Silk Weavers', p143.

16 *The Irish Times,* 11 Jul. 1911.

17 BMH WS 733 (James O'Shea); BMH WS 382 (Thomas Mallin).

18 Fox, R.M., *The History of the Irish Citizen Army*, Dublin, 1943, p90.

19 Lynch, Diarmuid, *The IRB and the 1916 Insurrection*, Cork, 1959, p70.

20 BMH WS 733, James O'Shea.

21 Nevin, Donal, *James Connolly: A Full Life*, Dublin, 2005, pp316-7; Ibid (ed.), *Between Comrades: James Connolly Letters and Correspondence 1889-1916*, Dublin, 2007, p622.

22 See for example: 'Events of Easter Week', *Catholic Bulletin*, Vol. VI, No. VII (July 1916), p393 and Ó Briain, Liam, 'Stephen's Green Area', *Capuchin Annual* (1966), p220.

23 *Inniu*, 14 Nov. 1966. One of these medals, for first prize and challenge cup in a fife and drum contest in March 1908, is now in the possession of the Kilmainham Gaol museum.

24 *The Irish Times*, 31 May 1913; Ibid, 6 Jun. 1913.

25 *Inniu*, 14 Nov. 1966.

26 Frank Robbins, *Under the Starry Plough: Recollections of the Irish Citizen Army*, Dublin, 1977; BMH WS 585 (Frank Robbins).

27 BMH WS 258 (Maeve Cavanagh).

28 *Inniu*, 7 Nov. 1966.

29 Ibid.

Chapter 4:

1 Padraig Yeates, *Lockout, Dublin 1913*, Dublin, 2000, ppxiii–xxiv.

2 *Dublin Evening Mail*, 13 Mar. 1913.

3 *Evening Telegraph*, 14 Mar. 1913.

4 Executive minutes of the Dublin Trades Council, 13 March 1913 (NLI: Ms. 12,782).

5 Ibid.

6 *Irish Worker*, 29 Mar. 1913.

7 Executive minutes of the Dublin Trades Council, 4 April 1913 (NLI: Ms. 12,782).

8 *Evening Telegraph*, 3 Apr. 1913.

9 *The Irish Times*, 5 Apr. 1913.

10 Minutes of the Dublin Trades Council, 7 April 1913 (NLI: Ms. 12,780).

11 *Irish Worker*, 12 Apr. 1913.

12 Ibid.

13 *Irish Worker*, 12 Apr. 1913.

14 Ibid.

15 Ibid.

16 Geraghty, Hugh, *William Patrick Partridge and his times: (1874-1917)*, Dublin, 2003, p171.

17 *Inniu*, 14 Nov. 1966.

18 *Evening Telegraph*, 9 Apr. 1913; *Dublin Evening Mail*, 9 Apr. 1913.

19 *The Irish Times*, 10 Apr. 1913.

20 *Dublin Evening Mail*, 10 Apr. 1913.

21 *The Irish Times*, 11 Apr. 1913.

22 *Dublin Evening Mail*, 11 Apr. 1913.

23 *Evening Telegraph*, 21 Apr. 1913.

24 Ibid, 22 Apr. 1913.

25 Minutes of the Dublin Trades Council, 5 May 1913 (NLI: Ms. 12,780).

26 *Irish Worker*, 10 May 1913.

27 Ibid, 31 May 1913.

28 *Evening Telegraph*, 2 Jun. 1913.

29 *Irish Worker*, 3 Jun. 1913.

30 *Evening Telegraph*, 3 Jun. 1913, *Dublin Evening Mail,* 3 Jun. 1913.

31 Minutes of the Dublin Trades Council, 16 June 1913 (NLI: Ms. 12,780A).

32 *Irish Worker*, 21 Jun. 1913.

33 Ibid, 10 May 1913.

34 Minutes of the Dublin Trades Council, 2 June 1913 (NLI: Ms. 12,780).

35 *Irish Worker*, 31 May 1913.

36 Ibid, 7 Jun. 1913.

Chapter 5:

1 *Inniu*, 14 Nov. 1921.

2 Fox, *Irish Citizen Army*, p. 91.

3 BMH WS 733 (James O'Shea).

4 Ibid.

5 Michael Mallin to Agnes Mallin, 7 May 1916 (Kilmainham Gaol Archive).

6 *Inniu*, 14 Nov. 1966.

7 Ibid.

8 *Bioscope*, 6 Jun. 1912; Ibid, 3 Oct. 1912.

9 *Irish Independent*, 15 Jun. 1915; Ibid, 22 Jun. 1915; *The Irish Times*, 22 Jun. 1915.

10 *Irish Worker*, 25 Apr., 1914.

11 Ibid, 2 May 1914.

12 Ibid, 9 May 1914.

13 Ibid, 6 Jun. 1914.

14 *Evening Telegraph*, 7 Aug. 1914; *The Irish Times*, 8 Aug. 1914; *Irish Independent*, 8 Aug. 1914.

15 Geraghty, *William Patrick Partridge*, p221.

16 BMH WS 733 (James O'Shea).

17 Minutes of the Irish Transport and General Workers' Union, No. 1 Branch, 5 May, 1915 (NLI Ms 7,298).

18 Ibid, 19 May 1915.

19 Ibid.

20 Minutes of ITGWU General Conference of delegates from all branches (NLI: Ms. 7,298).

21 *Inniu*, 7 Nov. 1966; Ibid, 14 Nov. 1966; Ibid, 21 Nov. 1966.

22 William Partridge to his wife, Lewes prison, 12 December 1916 (NLI: Ms. 2986).

23 O'Brien, Nora Connolly, *Portrait of a Rebel Father*, Dublin, 1935, p223.

Chapter 6:

1 For more information see Fox, *Irish Citizen Army* and *Dublin's Fighting Story*, pp52-60.

2 BMH WS 382 (Thomas Mallin).

3 See Fox, *Irish Citizen Army*, Chapter 7 'Fermenting Yeast' and Chapter 8 'Connolly Takes Command', pp84-100.

4 Charles Townshend, *Easter 1916: The Irish Rebellion*, London, 2005 edn., p111.

5 BMH WS 733 (James O'Shea).

6 *Evening Telegraph*, 2 Feb. 1914.

7 BMH WS 733 (James O'Shea); see also Fox, *Irish Citizen Army*, pp91-2.

8 Ibid.

9 Fox, *Irish Citizen Army*, p92.

10 BMH WS 919 (Ina Connolly).

11 O'Brien, Nora Connolly, *Portrait of a Rebel Father*, p.224.

12 Robbins, *Under the Starry Plough*, p70.

13 Fox, *Irish Citizen Army*, p178.

14 Robbins, *Under the Starry Plough*, p27.

15 BMH WS 733 (James O'Shea).

16 BMH WS 1666 (Thomas O'Donoghue).

17 Ibid.

18 *The Workers' Republic*, 4 Sept. 1915.

19 *The Workers' Republic*, 27 May 1915.

20 Robbins, *Under the Starry Plough*, p51-2; Fox, *Irish Citizen Army*, pp105-106.

21 Robbins, *Under the Starry Plough*, pp51-52; BMH WS 585 (Frank Robbins).

22 Robbins, *Under the Starry Plough*, p47.

23 BMH WS 733 (James O'Shea).

24 *Inniu*, 21 Nov. 1966.

25 BMH WS 258 (Maeve Cavanagh).

26 BMH WS 733 (James O'Shea).

27 Robbins, *Under the Starry Plough*, pp53-54.

28 *The Workers' Republic*, 29 May 1915.

29 Ibid, 7 Aug. 1915.

30 Ibid, 28 Aug. 1915.

31 Ibid, 9 Oct. 1915.

32 Ibid, 16 Oct. 1915.

33 Ibid, 28 Aug. 1915.

34 Ibid, 7 Aug. 1915.

35 Ibid, 16 Oct. 1915.

36 Ibid, 9 Oct. 1915.

37 Ibid, 16 Oct. 1915.

38 Ibid, 28 Aug. 1915.

39 Ibid, 9 Oct. 1915.

40 Ibid, 16 Oct. 1915.

41 BMH WS 733 (James O'Shea).

42 BMH WS 1766 (William O'Brien).

43 BMH WS 6 (Liam Ó Briain).

44 BMH WS 1766 (William O'Brien).

45 Robbins, *Under the Starry Plough*, p71.

46 BMH WS 6 (Liam Ó Briain).

47 BMH WS 733 (James O'Shea).

48 Lynch, *The IRB and the 1916 Insurrection*, pp124–126.

49 Ibid, pp94–95.

50 BMH 733 (James O'Shea).

Chapter 7:

1 McGarry, Fearghal, *The Rising: Ireland: Easter 1916*, Oxford, 2010, p106.

2 Robbins, *Under the Starry Plough*, p55.

3 BMH WS 733 (James O'Shea).

4 BMH WS 256 (Nellie Donnelly).

5 Frank Robbins statement, (NLI: MS 10,915); BMH WS 1666 (Thomas O'Donoghue).

6 Fox, *Citizen Army*, p137; Ibid, p136.

7 Extract from *Cuimhní Cinn*, published in *The Irish Times*, 16 Apr. 1962.

8 BMH WS 733 (James O'Shea).

9 BMH 421 (William Oman).

10 BMH WS 733 (James O'Shea).

11 Fox, *Citizen Army*, p137.

12 C. McDowell cited in Brian Barton, *From Behind a Closed Door: Secret Court Martial Records of the 1916 Easter Rising*, Belfast, 2002, p269.

13 BMH WS 733 (James O'Shea).

14 Ibid.

Chapter 8:

1 BMH WS 733 (James O'Shea). O'Shea states that he was originally assigned to the City Hall garrison but Mallin ordered him to stay with him and look after his kit and his 'personal comfort, whatever that meant' during the 'scrap'.

2 Ibid.

3 BMH WS 1666 (Thomas O'Donoghue).

4 Robbins, *Under the Starry Plough*, p84.

5 BMH WS 733 (James O'Shea).

6 Robbins, *Under the Starry Plough*, p86.

7 Ibid, p90.

8 Ibid, pp90–2.

9 Barton, Brian, and Foy, Michael, *The Easter Rising*, Belfast, 2004, pp89–90.

10 Liam Ó Briain, 'Stephen's Green Area'; BMH WS 269 (Harry Nicholls).

11 BMH WS 1666 (Thomas O'Donoghue).

12 Harry Nicholls remembers firing a shot from the College of Surgeons at some people who had returned on Tuesday to remove cars from a barricade in front of the building (BMH WS 269).

13 Robbins, *Under the Starry Plough*, p94.

14 'Easter Week Diary of Miss Lily Stokes', in Roger McHugh (ed), Dublin 1916 (Dublin, 1966), p. 65.

15 Ó Briain, 'Stephen's Green Area', p220.

16 Cited in McGarry, *The Rising*, p149.

17 Cited in Jeffery, Keith, *The GPO and the Easter Rising*, Dublin, 2006, p172.

18 Ibid, p180.

19 BMH WS 1666 (Thomas O'Donoghue).

20 BMH WS 733 (James O'Shea). O'Shea was later questioned by Mallin and Markievicz having been 'accused of being callous' by another witness to the shooting. He informed them that the 'morning would tell if I was right about spying.'

21 McGarry, *The Rising*, p137.

22 Robbins, *Under the Starry Plough*, p91.

23 Stephens, James, *The Insurrection in Dublin*, Dublin, 1916, p18.

24 Statement by W.G. Smith (NLI: MS 24,952).

25 Robbins, *Under the Starry Plough*, p86.

26 BMH WS 733 (James O'Shea).

27 Ibid.

28 'The Personal Experience of Miss L. Stokes, 11 Raglan Road, Dublin during the Sinn Féin Rebellion of 1916', Nonplus, 4 (Winter, 1960), p. 12.

29 Diary of Mrs George Coffey and Mr Diarmuid Coffey (NLI: MS 21,193); Statement by W.G. Smith, (NLI: MS 24,952).

30 Robbins, *Under the Starry Plough*, pp95-6; Frank Robbins statement (NLI: MS 10,915). They were unable to find the rifles. They were finally located on Thursday.

31 BMH WS 1666 (Thomas O'Donoghue).

32 Barton and Foy, *Easter Rising*, p93.

33 Collins, Lorcan, and Kostick, Conor, *The Easter Rising: A guide to Dublin in 1916*, Dublin, 2000, p74.

34 Ibid, pp107-8.

35 'Women in the Fight, a memoir by Constance de Markievicz' in McHugh, Roger (ed.), *Dublin 1916*, Dublin, 1966, p124.

36 *Irish Press*, 9 Apr. 1966.

37 Ó Briain, 'Stephen's Green Area', p225.

38 Barton and Foy, *Easter 1916*, p96.

39 BMH WS 733 (James O'Shea).

40 Ibid.

41 BMH WS 1666 (Thomas O'Donoghue).

42 W.G. Smith statement (NLI: MS 24,952).

43 BMH WS 733 (James O'Shea).

44 Ibid.

45 Robbins, *Under the Starry Plough*, p. 103; BMH WS 733 (James O'Shea).

46 *Irish Press* 9 Apr. 1966; William O'Brien recalls Mallin showing him his hat complete with two bullet holes in Richmond Barracks after the surrender (BMH WS 1766).

47 BMH WS 733 (James O'Shea).

48 Robbins, *Under the Starry Plough*, p. 106. Robbins felt 'very sore' about this intervention.

49 *Irish Press*, 9 Apr. 1966.

50 Barton and Foy, *Easter Rising*, p97.

51 Statement by W.G. Smith (NLI: MS 25,952).

52 Stephens, *Insurrection in Dublin*, p26.

53 Barton and Foy, *Easter Rising*, p99

54 Liam Ó Briain recalls one password as 'Wolfe Tone', Frank Robbins remembers 'Victory ninety-eight' as another.

55 Barton and Foy, *Easter Rising*, p99-100.

56 BMH WS 733 (James O'Shea).

57 Ibid.

58 Ó Briain, 'Stephen's Green Area', p229.

59 BMH WS 733 (James O'Shea); Robbins, *Under the Starry Plough*, pp109-110.

60 For reasons and analysis, see next chapter.

61 Robbins, *Under the Starry Plough*, pp113-4; BMH WS 733 (James O'Shea).

62 Ó Briain, 'Stephen's Green Area', p229, 231.

63 *Irish Press*, 9 Apr. 1966.

64 Robbins, *Under the Starry Plough*, pp117-8.

65 Ó Briain, 'Stephen's Green Area', p233.

66 Robbins, *Under the Starry Plough*, p. 117.

67 Collins and Kostick, *The Easter Rising*, p79.

68 BMH WS 733 (James O'Shea).

69 Liam Ó Briain, 'Stephen's Green Area', p231.

70 Ó Briain, 'Stephen's Green Area', p233.

71 BMH WS 296 (Harry Nicholls).

72 BMH WS 421 (William Oman).

73 In her Bureau of Military History statement it is recorded that Connolly gave her 'eight £10 notes', a truly remarkable sum of money given the circumstances. This is certainly

an error and she was more likely given eight ten-shilling notes or eight one-pound notes.

74 BMH WS 934 (Mary McLaughlin). Mrs Skeffington is Hanna Sheehy, wife of Francis.

75 'Women in the Fight', p. 124.

76 Ó Briain, 'Stephen's Green Area', p234.

77 Robbins, pp113, 119.

78 Ibid, p120.

79 BMH WS 1575 (William Oman).

80 Transcript of diary of Madeleine ffrench-Mullen, Kilmainham and Mountjoy Jails, 5-20 May 1916 (Allen Library, Box 201/File B); Robbins, *Under the Starry Plough*, p115.

81 BMH WS 1666 (Thomas O'Donoghue). Skinnider did, however, make a full recovery from her injuries.

82 Diary of Mrs George Coffey and Diarmuid Coffey, (NLI: MS 21,193).

83 Barton and Foy, *The Easter Rising*, p102.

84 Fox, *Citizen Army*, p165.

85 Ó Briain, 'Stephen's Green Area', p232.

86 Fox, *Citizen Army*, p167.

87 Townshend, Charles, *Easter 1916: The Irish Rebellion*, London, 2005, p260.

88 BMH WS 246 (Marie Perolz).

89 Barton and Foy, *Easter Rising*, p105.

90 Ibid.

91 Ó Briain, 'Stephen's Green Area', p234.

92 Barton and Foy, *Easter Rising*, p106.

93 MacLochlainn, Piarais (ed.), *Last Words: Letters and Statements of the Leaders Executed after the Rising at Easter 1916*, Dublin, 1990, p117.

94 *Dublin's Fighting Story*, Dublin, New Edition, 2009, p203.

95 BMH WS 1666 (Thomas O'Donoghue).

96 BMH WS 733 (James O'Shea).

97 Robbins, *Under the Starry Plough*, pp120-121.

98 BMH WS 733 (James O'Shea).

99 Robbins, *Under the Starry Plough*, pp122; BMH WS 1666 (Thomas O'Donoghue)

100 BMH WS 296 (Harry Nicholls).

101 BMH WS 1666 (Thomas O'Donoghue).

102 Townshend, *Easter 1916*, p251.

103 BMH WS 1575 (William Oman).

104 Ó Briain, 'Stephen's Green Area', p236.

105 Barton and Foy, *Easter Rising*, p109. James O'Shea (BMH WS 733) states that Mallin handed his sword over to Wheeler but Wheeler is likely correct in stating that it was a walking stick.

Chapter 9:

1 Barton, *From Behind a Closed Door*, pp28-32.

2 Ibid, p276.

3 Ibid.

4 *Irish Press*, 30 Apr. 1949.

5 Barton, *From Behind a Closed Door*, pp276-277.

6 Ibid, p278.

7 Ibid, p273.

8 Barton and Foy, *Easter Rising*, p358.

9 Barton, *From Behind a Closed Door*, p273.

10 Ibid.

11 Ibid, pp116, 146.

12 BMH WS 1574 (William Oman).

13 BMH WS 1766 (William O'Brien).

14 Barton, *From Behind a Closed Door*, p265.

15 Piarais F. MacLochlainn, *Last Words*, p121-2.

16 Ibid, pp150-1.

17 Account by Maurice Brennan (NLI: MS 10915); Memoirs of a female member of the Marrowbone Lane Garrison (NLI: MS 18556).

18 BMH WS 382 (Thomas Mallin); *Inniu*, 23 Oct. 1966.

19 *Irish Press*, 15 Jan. 1936.

20 *Inniu*, 23 Oct. 1966.

21 Ibid.

22 BMH WS 382 (Thomas Mallin).

23 Ibid.

24 BMH WS 382 (Thomas Mallin).

25 BMH WS 6 (Liam Ó Briain).

26 *Inniu*, 23 Oct. 1966.

27 MacLochlainn, *Last Words*, p127.

28 Fr Michael J. Heuston to James Brennan, 6 September 1965 (Kilmainham Gaol Museum).

29 *Catholic Bulletin*, Vol. VI, No. VII (July, 1916), pp399-400.

30 Barton, *From Behind a Closed Door*, p267.

31 MacLochlainn, *Last Words*, pp121-122.

32 Ibid, p122.

33 Ibid, p121.

34 Ibid, p123.

35 Original handwritten letter from Michael Mallin to Agnes Mallin, 7 May 1916 (Kilmainham Gaol Archive).

36 Ibid.

37 Ibid.

38 Ibid. Much of this passage was also removed by MacLochlainn.

39 *Inniu*, 23 Oct. 1966.

40 MacLochlainn, *Last Words*, p124.

41 Ibid, p123.

42 Ibid, pp123-124.

43 Ibid, p124.

44 *Catholic Bulletin*, Vol.VI, No.VII (July 1916), p399.

45 *Catholic Bulletin*, Vol.VI, No. XII (Dec. 1916), p700.

Chapter 10:

1 Barton and Foy, *Easter Rising*, p95.

2 BMH WS 907 (Laurence Nugent).

3 Ó Briain, 'St Stephen's Green Area', pp224-7.

4 BMH WS 907 (Laurence Nugent).

5 Barton and Foy, *Easter Rising*, p87.

6 F.X. Martin, '1916 – *Coup* d'état or 'bloody protest'?', *Studia Hibernica*, No 8 (1968), p113; Townshend, *Easter 1916*, pp101, 167.

7 Fox, *Citizen Army*, pp131-2.

8 Fox, R.M., 'Citizen Army Posts' in *Dublin's Fighting Story*, p107.

9 *Sunday Press*, 28 Apr. 1967; Ibid, 12 May 1967.

10 BMH WS 733 (James O'Shea); Fox, *Citizen Army*, p130.

11 Ibid, p32.

12 Jacob's was, in fact, occupied by a force of Irish Volunteers under the command of Thomas MacDonagh on Easter Monday.

13 Barton and Foy, *Easter Rising*, p98.

14 Martin, '1916', p113.

15 Townshend, *Easter 1916*, p167.

16 McGarry, *The Rising*, p130.

17 Ó Briain, 'Stephen's Green Area', p224; BMH WS 1666 (Thomas O'Donoghue).

18 Keith Jeffery, *Ireland and the Great War*, Cambridge, 2000, p51.

19 Max Caulfield, *The Easter Rebellion*, London, 1964, p97.

20 Barton and Foy, *Easter Rising* p90.

21 BMH WS 709 (Laurence Nugent).

22 Robbins, *Under the Starry Plough*, p100.

23 BMH WS 1666 (Thomas O'Donoghue).

24 Fox, *Citizen Army*, p. 145.

25 Townshend, p169.

26 Ibid, p8.

27 Ó Briain, 'Stephen's Green Area', p231.

28 Barton and Foy, *Easter Rising*, p92; Townshend, *Easter 1916*, pp 255–256.

29 Townshend, *Easter 1916*, p169.

30 BMH WS 907 (Laurence Nugent).

31 Barton and Foy, *Easter Rising*, p98.

32 BMH WS 6 (Liam Ó Briain).

33 *Irish Press*, 14 May 1935.

34 Transcript of diary of Madeleine ffrench-Mullen, Kilmainham and Mountjoy Jails, 5–20 May 1916 (Allen Library, Box 201/File B).

35 Ibid.

36 Extract from *Cuimhní Cinn*, published in *The Irish Times*, 17 Apr., 1952.

37 Ó Briain, 'Stephen's Green Area', p224; *An Muinteoir Náisiúnta*, Jul. 1966.

38 BMH WS 733 (James O'Shea).

39 Robbins, p103. Mallin later showed the bullet holes to William O'Brien in Richmond barracks.

40 Ó Briain, 'Stephen's Green Area' p231.

41 BMH WS 1666 (Thomas O'Donoghue).

42 BMH WS 733 (James O'Shea).

43 Townshend, *Easter 1916*, p181.

Chapter 11:

1 *The Irish Times*, 23 Apr. 2005.

2 Robbins, *Under the Starry Plough*, p65.

3 Irish National Volunteers Aid Association Dependants Fund Papers (NLI: Ms 24, 382).

4 Executive minutes of the INVAADF (NLI: Ms 23,469). Other sub-committees were formed to deal specifically with the American Relief Fund and to arrange employment for those who had lost jobs as a result of involvement, or suspicion of involvement, in the rebellion.

5 Ibid.

6 Ibid.

7 Irish National Volunteers Aid Association Dependants Fund Papers (NLI: Ms 24, 360).

8 Ibid.

9 *Catholic Bulletin*, Vol. 7 No. 12 (Dec. 1916), pp697-9.

10 Fr Joseph Mallin S.J., to the author, 10 Jan. 2008.

11 Executive minutes of the INDAAVF (NLI: Ms. 23,469).

12 Fr Joseph Mallin SJ to the author, 14 Jan. 2010.

13 William Partridge to his wife, Lewes prison, 12 Dec. 1916 (NLI: Ms. 2986).

14 *Prison Letters of Countess Markievicz*, London, 1987, p139.

15 Constance Markievicz to Eva Gore-Booth, Aylesbury prison, 21 September 1916 (NLI Ms. 5763).

16 *Prison Letters of Countess Markievicz*, p164.

17 Fr Joseph Mallin to the author, 1 April 2011; Fr Joseph Mallin to the author, 15 May 2011.

18 Irish National Volunteers Aid Association Dependants Fund Papers (NLI: Ms. 24,373).

19 Margaret Pearse to Agnes Mallin, 21 Sept. 1924 (in the possession of Fr Joseph Mallin S.J.).

20 *The Irish Times*, 23 Apr. 2005.

21 Fr Joseph Mallin to the author, 2 June 2011.

22 *Catholic Bulletin*, June 1932.

23 *The Irish Times*, 4 Apr. 1991.

24 Fr Joseph Mallin S.J. to the author, 5 May 2011.

25 *Irish Press*, 8 Jul. 1960; Ibid, 4 Feb. 1965.

26 *The Irish Times,* 25 Nov. 1922.

27 Fr Joseph Mallin S.J. to the author, 15 May 2011; *The Irish Times,* 19 Jun. 1982.

28 Fr Joseph Mallin, S.J., to the author, 24 June 2011.

29 *The Irish Times*, 2 Jul. 1982.

30 Austin Stack was an anti-Treaty IRA leader and later Minister for Defence; Seán Russell became Chief-of-Staff of the IRA and died returning to Ireland in a German submarine.

31 Fr Joseph Mallin to the author, 24 June 2011.

32 *The Irish Times*, 4 Apr. 1991.

33 Ferriter, Diarmaid, 'Commemorating the Rising, 1922-1965: "A figurative scramble for the bones of the patriot dead"?' Daly, Mary E., and O'Callaghan, Margaret (eds), *1916 in 1966: Commemorating the Easter Rising* (Dublin, 2007), pp199-200; 'Easter Week Commemorations' (NAI, Department of the Taoiseach S9815(A)).

34 Séamus Ó Mealláin to Taoiseach Éamon de Valera, 5 March 1941 (NAI: Department of the Taoiseach (DT) S9815 (A)); P.J. Long to Department of the Taoiseach, 18 March 1941 (Ibid).

35 *The Irish Times*, 2 Nov. 1966.

36 *The Sinn Féin Leaders of 1916*, Dublin, 1917.

37 Diary of Dr Kathleen Lynn, 8 December 1921.

38 Sean Lemass Election Poster, 1924 (Kilmainham Gaol archive).

Bibliography

PRIMARY SOURCES
Allen Library, Dublin

Indenture allowing Bartholomew Mallin
to become apprentice in the Dublin
silk trade.

Transcript of Madeleine ffrench-Mullen's
diary, 5-20 May 1916.

Kilmainham Gaol Archive, Dublin

Account Ledger of Michael Mallin, Royal
Scots Fusiliers.

Assorted memorabilia belonging to
Michael Mallin.

Correspondence with John Heuston
(Brother Michael).

Letter from Michael Mallin to Agnes
Mallin, 7 May 1916.

National Archives of Ireland, Dublin

1901 and 1911 Census of Ireland Records.

Department of the Taoiseach files, 'Easter
Commemorations'.

Duplicates of Bureau of Military History
Witness Statements.

National Archives, Kew, London

Military record of Michael Mallin, Royal
Scots Fusiliers.

National Library of Ireland, Dublin

Autograph narrative of W.G. Smith.

Baptism Records, Parish of St. Nicholas of
Myra (Without).

Diary of Mrs George Coffey and Mr
Diarmuid Coffey.

Dublin Trades Council Minute Books.

Florence O'Donoghue papers.

Irish Congress of Trade Unions Annual
Report 1913.

Letters from Dartmoor and Lewes prisons
from William Partridge to his wife.

Minute Book of the Irish Transport and
General Workers' Union, No. 1 Branch.

Prison letters of Countess Markievicz.

Two autographed letters from Michael
Mallin to Mrs J. Hickey.

Typescript narrative of Frank Robbins.

MISCELLANEOUS

Diary of Dr Kathleen Lynn.

Letters from Fr. Joseph Mallin S.J. to the
author.

Letters from Michael Mallin to Agnes
Hickey.

Sinn Féin Leaders of 1916 (pamphlet).

Newspapers and Periodicals

An Muinteoir Náisiúnta
Bioscope
Capuchin Annual
Catholic Bulletin
Dublin Evening Mail
Evening Herald
Evening Telegraph
Inniu
Irish Independent
Irish Press
Irish Times

Irish Worker

Nonplus

Studia Hibernica

Sunday Press

The Workers' Republic

Thom's Directory

Books and Articles

1916 Rebellion Handbook, Dublin, New Edition, 1998.

Barton, Brian, *From Behind a Closed Door: Secret Court Martial Records of the 1916 Easter Rising*, Belfast, 2002.

Barton, Brian, and Foy, Michael, *The Easter Rising*, Belfast, 2004.

Breathnach, Katherine, 'The Last of the Dublin Silk Weavers', *Irish Arts Review Yearbook* (1990/1991), pp134–43.

Buchan, John, *The History of the Royal Scots Fusiliers 1678-1918*, Oxford, 1925.

Campion, Mary, 'An Old Dublin Industry: Poplin', *Dublin Historical Record*, Vol. 19, No. 1 (December 1963), pp2–15.

Caulfield, Max, *The Easter Rebellion*, London, 1963.

Collins, Lorcan, and Kostick, Conor, *The Easter Rising: A Guide to Dublin in 1916*, Dublin, 2000.

Daly, Mary E., and O'Callaghan, Margaret (eds), *1916 in 1966: Commemorating the Easter Rising*, Dublin, 2007.

Dublin's Fighting Story 1916-1921, Dublin, New Edition, 2009.

Ferriter, Diarmaid, 'Commemorating the Rising, 1922-1965: "A figurative scramble for the bones of the patriot dead"?' in Daly, Mary E., and

O'Callaghan, Margaret (eds), *1916 in 1966: Commemorating the Easter Rising*, Dublin, 2007.

Fox, R.M., *The History of the Irish Citizen Army*, Dublin, 1944.

Geraghty, Hugh, *William Patrick Partridge and His Times: (1874-1917)*, Dublin, 2003.

Jeffery, Keith, *Ireland the Great War*, Cambridge, 2000.

Jeffrey, Keith, *The GPO and the Easter Rising*, Dublin, 2006.

Lynch, Diarmuid, *The IRB and the 1916 Insurrection*, Cork, 1959.

MacLochlainn, Piaras F., *Last Words: Letters and Statements of the Leaders Executed after the Rising at Easter 1916*, Dublin, 1990.

Martin, F.X. (ed.), *Leaders and Men of the Easter Rising*, London, 1967.

Martin, F.X., 'The 1916 Rising – A *Coup d'état* or a "Bloody protest"?', *Studia Hibernica*, 8 (1968).

Matthews, Ann, *Renegades: Irish Republican Women*, Dublin, 2010.

Matthews, Ann, 'Vanguards of the Revolution? The Irish Citizen Army in 1916' in O'Donnell, Ruán (ed), *The impact of the 1916 Rising among the nations*, Dublin, 2008.

Prison Letters of Countess Markievicz, London, 1987.

McGarry, Fearghal, *The Rising: Ireland: Easter 1916*, Oxford, 2010.

McHugh, Roger (ed), *Dublin 1916*, Dublin, 1966.

Nevin, Donal, *Between Comrades: Letters and Correspondence of James Connolly*

1889-1916, Dublin, 2007.

Nevin, Donal, *James Connolly: A Full Life,* Dublin, 2005.

Nowlan, Kevin B. (ed.), *The Making of 1916: Studies in the History of the Rising,* Dublin, 1969.

Ó Briain, Liam, 'Stephen's Green Area', *Capuchin Annual* (1966), pp219-236.

O'Brien, Nora Connolly, *Portrait of a Rebel Father* , Dublin, 1935.

O'Connor Lysaght, D.R., 'The Irish Citizen Army, 1913-1916: White, Larkin and Connolly', *History Ireland,* Vol. 14, No.2, 1916: 90th Anniversary Issue (Mar. – Apr., 2006), pp16-2.

O'Donnell, Ruán (ed), *The Impact of the 1916 Rising among the Nations,* Dublin, 2008.

Prunty, Jacinta, *Dublin Slums 1800-1925: A Study in Urban Geography,* Dublin, 1998.

Robbins, Frank, 'Remembering Easter Week 1916', *Dublin Historical Record,* Vol. 23, No 2/3 (December, 1969), pp95-100.

Robbins, Frank, *Under the Starry Plough: Recollections of the Irish Citizen Army,* Dublin, 1977.

Shiels, Damian, 'The Archaeology of Insurrection: St. Stephen's Green, 1916', *Archaeology Ireland,* Vol. 20, No. 1 (Spring 2006), pp6-11.

Stephens, James, *Insurrection in Dublin,* Dublin, 1916.

Townshend, Charles, *Easter 1916: The Irish Rebellion,* London, 2005.

Yeates, Padraig, *Lockout: Dublin 1913,* Dublin, 2000.

Index